OZ CLARKE

250
BEST
WINES
WINE BUYING GUIDE
2009

PAVILION

First published in 2008 by Pavilion Books
An imprint of
Anova Books Company Ltd
10 Southcombe Street
London W14 0RA

www.anovabooks.com
www.ozclarke.com

Editor Maggie Ramsay
Cover design Georgina Hewitt
Design Nichola Smith
DTP Jayne Clementson
Tastings and database assistance Matthew Jones, Sarah Richards

A CIP catalogue for this book is available from the British Library
ISBN 978-1-862-058279

10 9 8 7 6 5 4 3 2 1
Printed and bound in Italy by G. Canale & C. spa

The information and prices contained in this book were correct to the best of our knowledge when we went to press. Although every care has been taken in the preparation of this book, neither the publishers nor the editors can accept any liability for any consequences arising from the use of information contained herein.

Oz Clarke 250 Best Wines is an annual publication.
We welcome any suggestions you might have for the next edition.

Acknowledgments

We would like to thank all the retailers, agents and individuals who have helped to source wine labels and bottle photographs.

Please bear in mind that wine is not made in infinite quantities – some of these may well sell out, but the following year's vintage should then become available. Prices are those that applied in summer 2008. All prices listed are per 750ml bottle inclusive of VAT, unless otherwise stated. Remember that some retailers only sell by the case – which may be mixed.

Contents

Introduction

I've just found a new reason to visit public lavatories. It's to see if they've installed a Dyson Airblade. This is a completely brilliant hand dryer. You put your hands into the cavity and they're **attacked by a ferocious blast of air**: they're dry in a couple of seconds. It's fun, it's fantastically efficient, and it saves 80% of the carbon emissions per hand-dry. The point is, hand dryers as a category haven't seen any innovation for donkey's years. Suddenly this invention comes along and transforms the category. Innovation. The buzzword of business. And it's currently an obsession of the wine world. Well, it's a 21st-century obsession. It's not that long ago that words like tradition, experience, heredity were used to demonstrate quality and character – even when they weren't remotely relevant, like the big Californian brands implying that they were made by **nice old men in rocking chairs** gazing out over wooded hillsides and valleys full of rustling vines. I wish. Now it's innovation. Flavoured wines. Coloured wines. Wines with silly names that scream '*don't* buy me' to serious wine drinkers. But, of course, it isn't serious wine drinkers the crazed marketeers are targeting. Take 'Pink Chardonnay Frizzante' for instance. Here's a snippet from the marketing blurb: 'Customers in the UK are increasingly buying into rosé and sparkling wine categories, while Chardonnay remains one of the most popular grape varieties.' All true. Rosé wine sales are booming, and more good ones are reaching the market each year. **Sparkling wines, yes, we're drinking more and more.** Chardonnay. Gosh. The best-known grape variety. Bingo. The fact that Chardonnay is a white grape seems to have escaped them.

I don't think the wine world needs more silly innovations, but I *do* think that in the last generation or so there have been great innovations, sometimes through the genius and inspiration of winemakers, sometimes through the relentless desire of men and women, particularly in the New World, to push back the geographical boundaries into areas where grapegrowing was regarded as impossible. Australia's Chardonnay revolutionized commercial, big-volume, easily available white wine. New Zealand Sauvignon Blanc changed the world too, by creating **a flavour of unheard-of pungency and tangy brilliance** that the whole world has been trying to emulate ever since. Thirty-five years ago, New Zealand's South Island was vineless. Cloudy Bay, possibly the world's trendiest white wine, had its first vintage in 1985. Chile, with its deep, lush, ripe fruit quality, especially in Merlots and Cabernets, changed the way we thought of big-volume, widely available reds during the 1990s. *This* is the innovation we wine drinkers want.

But I, for one, don't crave change for the sake of it. New Zealand Sauvignon has defined the tangy, refreshing white wine style for more than a decade. Recently, though, more and more of them have seemed to lack zip, to be sweeter, flatter, short on that brilliant pungency that made them famous. I know that some of our supermarket buyers have been asking them to increase their sugar levels to broaden their appeal. Appeal to whom? People who don't like pungency? **Let them drink Pinot Grigio**. And I know that certain wine competitions have been showering gold medals on fat, sweet, alcoholic travesties of Sauvignon which then encourages others to think that's the way forward. New Zealand Sauvignon wasn't doing anything wrong, it was doing everything right. Nothing was broken, nothing needed fixing. And here's the rub. One of our most powerful and best High Street wine buyers told me this week he had a feeling in his gut that the UK was beginning to tire of the onslaught of Sauvignon led by New Zealand. His gut is usually right. He's off to Italy to source more of their intriguing dry whites. Italy! If New Zealand, and Sauvignon in general, wants to hold on to its premier position, then going back to basics would be a good start.

We could all help by paying a proper price for our wine. That 14p duty increase in April's Budget is a consumer tax. We're consumers; we should pay it. But we have **a very strange relationship** in this country with wine and the price we're prepared to pay. In 2007 the average price for a bottle of wine finally scraped past £4 to £4.01. In 1998 the price was £3.45. So that's 56p in 10 years. If we take inflation into account, the average price *should* now be somewhere around £4.50. And what about duty? Well, between 1998 and 2007 duty went up 37p a bottle, and this year's 14p brings that to 51p. Add that to the average price and **it should be over a fiver** just to stand still. But it's only just crept past £4. And in the supermarkets – where 80% of us buy our wine – the average price in 2007 was £3.84.

Before we start crowing and saying **didn't we do well**, let's pause. When the price of bread goes up, we pay. Milk, butter, eggs, bacon, petrol ... we grumble, but we pay. This year particularly, all the things necessary to make wine, bottle it and get it to our table, have all gone up – just as they have for every other item in our shopping basket. Oil has doubled in price per barrel, and that affects energy at every stage of the process: glass, labels, bottling lines, cardboard boxes, transport. Growing grapes? More expensive too. And yet we still expect our wine to be cheap. The big retailers said that the 'buy one get one free' (BOGOF) mechanism – or scourge, in my view – was no longer valid in credit crunch times. They stopped this **discount junkies' fix** for, oh, several weeks, until one of our biggest supermarkets flooded the floor with BOGOFs and everyone else said it would be commercial suicide not to join in. I tell you who it's suicide for: the growers and producers. Supermarket margins don't suffer with these discount promotions – the money is clawed back from producers. Then we wonder why the big brands taste of so little: the producers have to keep cheapening the blend just to keep doing business in the UK. Other producers simply decide to send their better wines to countries where people are more aware of the effort and investment that goes into making good wine. Until we stop falling for these deep discount tactics the quality will get worse, and from being the proudly beating heart of the world wine trade, **the UK will become a dumping ground for plonk**.

That's why this guide is here. To seek out what's good in the High Street and the supermarkets and to encourage our swelling legions of independent retailers to keep up their spirits. *Their* average price is nearer £8 a bottle, and in their shops **£7.99 really means £7.99 worth of wine.**

In any case, the mood of the world is changing. The severe price rises in all areas caused by the global chaos in 2008 aren't all bad. They will make us **focus more closely on what we buy and what we pay**. In particular, climate change is forcing us to take a greener view of life, and we are increasingly having to accept that this doesn't come cheap. Wine is a reasonably responsible industry at the production end. In decent vineyards fewer and fewer chemicals are used; in decent wineries resources are being carefully utilized and recycled as never before. But wine does come in heavy glass, and it often comes a very long way. Glass and packaging produce far more carbon emissions than the wine does. Are we prepared to change? Some glass manufacturers I spoke to said that beer drinkers, cider drinkers, whisky, brandy, gin drinkers were happy to buy lighter glass bottles without feeling they were buying a cheaper product. Only wine drinkers saw a heavier bottle as a sign of quality and resisted lighter bottles. So it's up to us to **reject any spuriously heavy bottles** and accept that lighter glass doesn't mean worse wine. But it's also up to some serious producers whose quality we trust to commit to lighter glass. Things are moving. In the past two years, the use of lighter glass has reduced UK glass weight by 11,400 tonnes a year, and recycled glass has increased by 24,000 tonnes a year. Add to that the increase of wine being imported in bulk and bottled here – 199 million bottles are now filled here, not at source, that's 79 million bottles more than two years ago – and we are beginning to play our part. And we must continue to do so. Climate change is real. It's going to transform our lives. You don't get level-headed guys like Miguel Torres, head of the great Spanish winemaking dynasty, buying land 1500 metres up in the Pyrenees for fun. There are no vines there. The land isn't even suitable. Yet. But it will be. In 20 years he'll be growing his white grapes there. Unless he's in England. Every farmer, every grapegrower will attest to climate change. It has radically changed the options for winemakers in England. Take advantage of it while you can. Professor Richard Selley of Imperial College, Britain's greatest expert on climate change in our winelands, says climate change is likely to become so severe within 75 years that cool-climate varieties will have migrated as far north as Loch Ness, **Yorkshire will be producing Shiraz and Viognier**, and parts of the Thames Valley, the Severn Valley and Hampshire will be so hot they'll only be fit for raisins. Fanciful? Maybe. Maybe not.

Wine finder

Shiraz, Jindalee Circle Collection, Jindalee/Littore Family Estate, South Eastern Australia 90
Shiraz, Sanguine Estate, Heathcote, Victoria 32
Shiraz, Selkirk, Bremerton Wines, Langhorne Creek, South Australia 60
Shiraz, Shaw & Smith, Adelaide Hills, South Australia 20
Shiraz, Twins, Maverick Wines, Barossa Valley, South Australia 21
Shiraz, Water Wheel Vineyards, Bendigo, Victoria 62
Shiraz-Cabernet, Jindu, South Eastern Australia 100
Shiraz-Viognier, Zonte's Footstep, Langhorne Creek, South Australia 72
Tempranillo Reserve, Tim Adams, Clare Valley, South Australia 25

Pink
Sangiovese Rosé, Eldredge Vineyards, Clare Valley, South Australia 103

Sweet
Fine Old Muscat, Buller, Victoria 126
Orange Muscat & Flora, Brown Brothers, Victoria 127

Sparkling
Jansz Rosé, Yalumba, Tasmania 119

AUSTRIA
White
Grüner Veltliner, Langenloiser Berg Vogelsang, Weingut Bründlmayer, Kamptal 25

Grüner Veltliner, Obere Steigen, Weingut Huber, Traisental 46
Grüner Veltliner, Wachtberg, Salomon Undhof, Kremstal 44

CHILE
White
Chardonnay, Special Cuvée, Montes Alpha, Casablanca Valley 42
Chardonnay, The Society's Chilean, Concha y Toro, Casablanca Valley 84
Chilean Chardonnay, Valle Central (Asda) 98
Sauvignon Blanc, Garuma Vineyard, Viña Leyda, Leyda Valley 24
Sauvignon Blanc, Limited Selection, Montes, Leyda Valley 54
Sauvignon Blanc, Reserva, Montes, Casablanca Valley 58
Sauvignon Blanc, Viña Tabali, Limarí Valley 58
Sauvignon Blanc, Vision, Cono Sur, Casablanca Valley 44
Viognier, Anakena, Rapel Valley 49
Viognier-Riesling-Chardonnay, Ona, Anakena, Rapel Valley 50

Red
Cabernet Sauvignon, Casillero del Diablo, Concha y Toro, Central Valley 78
Cabernet Sauvignon, Luis Felipe Edwards, Colchagua Valley 87
Cabernet Sauvignon Reserva, El Huique, Colchagua Valley 75

Cabernet Sauvignon-Carmenère, Porta Reserva, Viñedos y Bodegas Córpora 88
Carmenère, Adobe, Viñedos Emiliana, Colchagua Valley 76
Carmenère, Gamma, Viñedos Emiliana, Colchagua Valley 79
Carmenère, Los Robles, Fairtrade, Curico Valley 92
Carmenère, Punto Niño, Laroche, Colchagua Valley 76
Coyam, Viñedos Emiliana, Colchagua Valley 37
Palo Alto Reserva, Maule Valley 67
Pinot Noir, Reserva, Cono Sur, Casablanca Valley 74
Pinot Noir, Winemaker Reserva, Porta, Viñedos y Bodegas Córpora, Bío Bío Valley 77
Pinot Noir-Merlot, Ona, Anakena, Casablanca Valley 67
Syrah, Apalta Vineyard, Montes Alpha, Colchagua Valley 60
Syrah, Reserva, Viña Falernia, Elqui Valley 20

Pink
Merlot Rosé, Los Robles, Fairtrade, Curicó Valley 107

Sweet
Cantavida, Late Harvest, Limarí Valley 127

ENGLAND
White
Bacchus, Chapel Down, Kent 46

Sparkling

Balfour Brut Rosé, Kent 114
Bloomsbury, Ridgeview, West Sussex 118
English Sparkling Rosé, Chapel Down, Kent 119

FRANCE
VdP = Vin de Pays
White

Bordeaux Blanc, Ch. Le Grand Verdus 45
Chablis Premier Cru Beauroy, Dom. Jean-Marie Naulin, Burgundy 38
Chenin-Chardonnay, VdP des Côtes de Gascogne, Dom. du Tariquet, South-West France 86
Colombard-Ugni Blanc, VdP des Côtes de Gascogne, Beaulieu, South-West France 84
VdP des Côtes de Gascogne, La Courtine, Producteurs Plaimont, South-West France 84
VdP des Côtes de Gascogne, Harmonie de Gascogne, Dom. de Pellehaut, South-West France 86
Côtes du Rhône, Dom. de la Bastide, Rhône Valley 59
VdP du Gers, Vieille Fontaine, Plaimont/Producteurs Vignoble de Gascogne, South-West France 97
Gewürztraminer, Taste the Difference (Cave de Turckheim), Alsace 57
Graves, Berry's Own Selection, Extra Ordinary White, Bordeaux 34

Gringet, Les Alpes, Vin de Savoie, D & P Belluard, Savoie 35
Mâcon-Chardonnay (Adnams Selection White Burgundy), Cuvée Paul Talmard, Dom. Talmard 57
Muscadet Sèvre et Maine sur lie, Taste the Difference (Dom. Jean Douillard), Loire Valley 85
Riesling, Grand Cru Eichberg, Philippe Zinck, Alsace 24
Rolle, VdP des Coteaux de Murviel, Dom. de Coujan, Languedoc 59
Sauvignon Blanc, Dom. Octavie, Touraine, Loire Valley 54
Viognier, Vent di Damo, VdP des Portes de Mediterranée, les Terrasses d'Eole, Languedoc 55
Vouvray, Aigle Blanc, Prince Poniatowski, Loire Valley 39
Xavier, Vin de Table 50

Red

Beaujolais (Asda) 100
Beaujolais, Cuvée des Vignerons, Cave des Vignerons de Bully, Burgundy 92
Brouilly, Ch. du Pavé, Beaujolais 61
Carignan, Old Vines, VdP de l'Aude, Le Sanglier de la Montagne, les Caves du Mont Tauch, Languedoc 99
Carignan, Old Vine, VdP de l'Aude, Cuvée Christophe, Dom. de la Souterranne, Languedoc 65
Chiroubles, Ch. de Javernand, Beaujolais 63

Claret – The Best (Morrisons), Sichel, Bordeaux 91
Corbières, Ch. Pech-Latt, Languedoc 76
Corbières, Réserve de la Perrière, les Caves du Mont Tauch, Languedoc 99
Cornas, Grandes Bastides, Tardieu Laurent, Rhône Valley 34
Côte de Brouilly, Dom. Georges Viornery, Beaujolais 65
Coteaux du Languedoc, Terrasses du Larzac, Mas des Brousses 26
Coteaux du Vendômois, Dom. de Montrieux, Loire Valley 61
Côtes du Rhône, Ch. les Quatre Filles, Rhône Valley 66
Côtes du Rhône Villages, Taste the Difference (M Chapoutier), Rhône Valley 88
Côtes du Ventoux, L'Archange, Dom. des Anges, Rhône Valley 63
Entraygues-le Fel, Olivier et Laurent Mousset, South-West France, 70
Faugères, Le 1er, Ch. Haut Lignières, Languedoc 79
VdP du Gard, Saint Roche, Dom. de Tavernel, Languedoc 89
VdP de l'Hérault, Cuvée Chasseur, les Producteurs Réunis 101
Lirac, Dom. du Joncier, Rhône Valley 67
Merlot, VdP de l'Aude, Cuvée Guillaume, Dom. de la Souterranne, Languedoc 77

Minervois La Livinière, La Cantilène, Ch. Sainte-Eulalie, Languedoc 64

VdP d'Oc, Pontificis, Grenache-Syrah-Mourvedre, Laurent Delaunay, Languedoc 77

VdP des Portes de Mediterranée, Manjo Fango, les Terrasses d'Eole, Languedoc 73

Saint Chinian, Ch. Bousquette, Languedoc 74

Syrah, VdP de l'Ardèche, Cave Saint-Désirat, Rhône Valley 93

VdP de Vaucluse, Les Rives d'Alcion, Dom. André Brunel, Languedoc 93

Xavier, Vin de Table 68

Pink

Beaujolais Rosé, Dom. de Grandmont 104

Coteaux du Languedoc, Mescladis, Dom. Clavel 106

Coteaux du Languedoc, Nord Sud, Laurent Miquel 104

VdP des Côtes de Gascogne, Harmonie de Gascogne, Dom. de Pellehaut, South-West France 107

Côtes de Provence, Les Fenouils, Dom. de Jale 103

Côtes de Provence, MiP – Made in Provence, Dom. Sainte Lucie 103

Côtes du Rhône Rosé, Cuvée Prestige, Sainsbury's (Les Vignerons de l'Enclave des Papes), Rhône Valley 106

Languedoc Rosé, VdP d'Oc, Asda Extra Special (JC Mas) 107

Mâcon Rosé, M&S (Cave de Prissé), Burgundy 105

Sweet

Jurançon, Chamarré Tradition, South-West France 126

Ultime Récolte, Jeff Carrel 125

Sparkling

Champagne, Blanc de Blancs Brut, Delamotte 114

Champagne, Blanc de Blancs Brut, Waitrose (P&C Heidsieck) 117

Champagne, Brut Tradition Grand Cru, Ambonnay, Egly-Ouriet 115

Champagne, Brut Zero, Tarlant 115

Champagne, De Brissar 116

Champagne, Cuvée Brut, Oudinot 118

Champagne, Premier Cru, Blanc de Blancs Brut, De Saint Gall 116

Champagne, Premier Cru, Duval-Leroy 116

Champagne, Premier Cru, Pierre Vaudon 117

Champagne, Premier Cru, Rilly La Montagne, Philippe Brugnon 117

Crémant de Bourgogne, Grande Reserve, Perle de Vigne, Louis Bouillot, Burgundy 119

Crémant de Limoux, Cuvée Saint Laurent, Georges et Roger Antech, Languedoc 120

GERMANY
White

Riesling, Blue Slate, Dr Loosen, Mosel 52

Riesling, Steillage, Tesco Finest, Mosel 82

Riesling Kabinett, Piesporter Goldtröpfchen, Weingut Kurt Hain, Mosel 45

Riesling Kabinett, Trierer Deutschherrenberg, Deutschherrenhof, Mosel 83

Riesling Kabinett, Ürziger Würzgarten, Dr Loosen, Mosel 39

Silvaner Kabinett, Trocken, Würzburger Abtsleite, Juliusspital, Franken 45

Sweet

Scheurebe Beerenauslese, Dürkheimer Spielberg, Darting Estate, Pfalz 125

HUNGARY
White

Pinot Grigio, Hilltop Neszmély (M&S) 86

ITALY
White

Greco, Le Ralle, Alovini, Basilicata 56

Greco di Tufo, Feudi di San Gregorio, Campania 37

Pecorino, Terre di Chieti, Colle dei Venti, Caldora, Abruzzo 43

Soave Classico, Calvarino, Pieropan, Veneto 22

Verdicchio dei Castelli di Jesi Classico, Moncaro, Marche 96

Verdicchio di Matelica, Colle
Stefano, Marche 56
Villa Antinori, Tuscany 55
Red
Barbera d'Alba, Conca del Grillo,
Silvano Bolmida, Piedmont 63
Barbera d'Alba, Josetta Saffirio,
Piedmont 37
Carso, Teran, Zidarich, Friuli-Venezia
Giulia 32
Il Fagiano, Vino da Tavola Rosso 89
La Grola, Allegrini, Veneto 26
Montepulciano d'Abruzzo, Torre
Scalza (M&S), Abruzzo 70
Salice Salentino, Feudi di San
Marzano, Puglia 87
Salice Salentino, La Masseria,
Cantine di San Marzano, Puglia
90
Teroldego delle Venezie, Novello
delle Vivene, Trentino 74
Valpolicella, Allegrini, Veneto 68
Pink
Pinot Grigio Superiore, Ramato,
Breganze, Cantina Beato
Bartolomeo da Breganze, Veneto
105
Sweet
Recioto di Soave, Vigna Marogne,
Tamellini, Veneto 124
Sparkling
Prosecco di Conegliano-
Valdobbiadene, La Marca, Veneto
120

NEW ZEALAND
White
Chardonnay, Private Bin, Villa Maria,
East Coast 57
Sauvignon Blanc, Boreham Wood,
Clark Estate, Awatere Valley,
Marlborough 43
Sauvignon Blanc, Clifford Bay
Reserve, Villa Maria, Marlborough
29
Sauvignon Blanc, Dashwood,
Vavasour, Marlborough 53
Sauvignon Blanc, Explorers Vineyard,
Marlborough 56
Sauvignon Blanc, Goldwater,
Marlborough 49
Sauvignon Blanc, Matahiwi Estate,
Wairarapa 51
Sauvignon Blanc, Origin, Grove Mill,
Marlborough 47
Sauvignon Blanc, Sandy Ridge,
Seifried, Nelson 51
Sauvignon Blanc, Shepherds Ridge
(Wither Hills), Marlborough 49
Sauvignon Blanc, The Reach,
Vavasour, Marlborough 54
Sauvignon Blanc, Villa
Maria/Waitrose, Marlborough
51

PORTUGAL
White
Vinho Verde, Quinta de Azevedo 83
Red
Dão, Quinta de Saes 72

Tinta da Ânfora, VR Alentejano,
Bacalhôa Vinhos de Portugal 78
Port
10 year old Tawny Port (M&S) 134
Crusted Port, Graham's 133
Crusted Port, The Society's
Exhibition 135
Late Bottled Vintage, Fonseca 135
Late Bottled Vintage Port, Graham's
136
LBV Niepoort 134
Pink Port (M&S) 136
Reserve Port (M&S) 136

SLOVENIA
White
Furmint, Verus Vineyards, Ormoz
52

SOUTH AFRICA
White
Sauvignon Blanc, De Grendel,
Tijgerberg, Cape of Good Hope 53
Sauvignon Blanc, Fryer's Cove,
Bamboes Bay 28
Sauvignon Blanc, Stellar Organics,
Fairtrade, Western Cape 85
Sauvignon Blanc, Vergelegen,
Stellenbosch 50
Red
Cabernet-Shiraz (Swartland Winery)
100
Pinotage, The Best (Morrisons) 75
Syrah, TMV Tulbagh Mountain
Vineyards, Swartland 39

Pink

Brampton Rosé, Rustenberg, Coastal Region 106

Merlot Rosé, Reserve Selection, Ormer Bay, Fairtrade, Western Cape 105

Slowine Rosé, Overberg 105

Sweet

Weisser Riesling Noble Late Harvest, Paul Cluver, Elgin 126

SPAIN

White

Rías Baixas, O Rosal, Bodegas Terras Gauda, Galicia 22

Sauvignon-Verdejo, Casa del Sol, Agricola Castellana, Castilla y León 85

Red

Abadia Retuerta, Selección Especial, Vino de la Tierra de Castilla y León 28

Campo de Borja Tinto, Gran López, Crianzas y Viñedos Santo Cristo, Aragón 99

Garnacha, Gran Tesoro, Bodegas Borsao, Campo de Borja, Aragón 101

Garnacha, Vineyard X, Bodegas Borsao, Aragón 92

Ribera del Duero, El Quintanal, Quintana del Pidio, Castilla y León 71

Ribera del Duero, Roble, Dominio Basconcillos, Castilla y León 38

Rioja Tinto Crianza, Viña Caña 88

Rioja, Clisos, Federico Paternina 64

Rioja, Zuazo Gaston 91

Rioja Reserva, Contino 33

Rioja Reserva, Elegia, Taste the Difference (Torre de Oña) 65

Tempranillo, Gazur, Telmo Rodríguez, Ribera del Duero 68

Tempranillo-Cabernet Sauvignon, Sequiot, Valencia 91

Sweet

Alicante, Moscatel, Casta Diva, Cosecha Miel, Bodegas Gutiérrez de la Vega 124

Moscatel de Valencia (Asda) 127

Sparkling

Cava Brut, Vineyard X, Covides 121

Cava Rosado Brut, Mas Miralda 121

Cava Rosé Brut (Somerfield) 121

Cava Vintage Brut (M&S)120

Gotas de Plata Rosé, Viñedos y Reservas, La Mancha 121

Fortified

Fino del Puerto, Solera Jerezana, Waitrose/Emilio Lustau 132

Fino Muy Seco, Tio Pepe, González Byass 131

Manzanilla Mariscal (Tanners) 132

Manzanilla, Las Medallas de Argüeso 133

Manzanilla Pasada, Pastrana, Bodegas Hidalgo La Gitana 131

Oloroso Dulce Viejo, Matusalem, González Byass 131

Oloroso Muy Viejo, Bodegas Tradición 130

Palo Cortado Muy Viejo, Apostoles, González Byass 130

USA

White

Chardonnay, Saintsbury, Carneros, California 30

Red

Cabernet Sauvignon, Cycles Gladiator, Central Coast, California 69

Petite Syrah, Teichert Ranch, Lodi, California 71

Syrah, Cerro Romauldo, Marmesa Vineyards, Edna Valley 62

Syrah, Cline Cellars, California 72

Zinfandel, De Loach, California 69

Index of producers/brands

TOP
250

**TOP
40**

This hasn't been an easy year for wine. After years of positive media coverage, politicians have suddenly decided that suburban Shiraz drinkers are a soft target and are unlikely to react violently if abused, slandered and over-taxed. And I suppose they're right. Just open another bottle of Shiraz with our friends and moan about the government. 'Twas ever thus. But if we are to feel beleaguered, let's make sure that what we drink is filled with character and individuality. Let's not just blithely believe the marketing blather and glossy ads that companies spend their money on rather than flavours in the bottle – let's go for the original and unique. The following selection is of wines that I have *loved* this year – not just liked, or respected, but truly been bowled over by. They're from big companies and small, famous producers and unknowns, grapes and regions that are commonplace and obscure. But they all have one thing in common. They're made with passion and with pride by men and women who wouldn't know how to make a dull wine, and would throw you out of their cellars if you asked them to.

This chapter lists my favourite wines of the year, both red and white:

♠ = red wine   ◊ = white wine

1 2005 Syrah, Reserva, Viña Falernia, Elqui Valley, Chile, 14% ABV

◆ Great Western Wine, £9.95

This was just a rumour long before it was a flavour, a perfume, a stain in the glass, a mellow reflection on pleasure drained. The rumour said that up in the far north of Chile, towards the Atacama desert, the driest place in the world – far too arid to grow a decent vine – someone was producing cool-climate reds of succulence and scent and restrained beauty that would make the greatest vineyards of France purple with envy. Cool climate? In the desert? Well, this is the genius of Chile. Bounded by ice-cold Antarctic currents, the hotter the inland gets, the fiercer and colder the winds that will rip up the coastal valleys towards the heat. The Elqui valley, the baked interior, the hissing chill of the sea gales. Sun for ripeness, cool for fruit and perfume and beauty. A star was being born in the far north. If French wines can boast that their texture is superior to those of the New World, here's where the argument begins to break down. This wine has fantastic texture. The fruit is dense yet soft, with real intensity, the tannin there to season not to bully, and the wine rolls across your tongue, leaving an eiderdown of glycerine that fails to smother the tingling trail of acid and grainy tannin. Just as the lush blackberry and licorice concentration fails to silence the fringe flavours of pepper, celery, herbs and woodsmoke. And the price? £9.95. That's *also* the genius of Chile. Wonderful flavours, prices we can afford.

2 2006 Shiraz, Shaw & Smith, Adelaide Hills, South Australia, 14.5% ABV

◆ Bennetts, Liberty Wines, Wimbledon Wine Cellars, Noel Young, £17.99

This Shiraz has got more in common with Chile's great cool-climate Falernia (my number one wine, above) than the majority of Aussie Shirazes. Especially the majority of South Australian Shirazes, because that's the home of the big Barossa Beast and the McLaren Monster. Shaw & Smith never wanted to make the kind of overripe style that has unfortunately become popular recently elsewhere in Australia. They started life making Sauvignon and unoaked Chardonnay in the damp hills above Adelaide, and they haven't forgotten their roots. So when a few cultured palates started rebelling against the excesses of the Barossa, Shaw & Smith already had a vision of cool-climate Shiraz, an idea of where to grow the grapes, and an idea of how to make

it. And their efforts have been a triumphant success. The wine is vibrant and dark with a smell of sweet-sour black cherry and fresh farm cream. That black cherry runs right through the wine, picking up crunchy white pepper, celery, licorice and Valrhona-type dark chocolate along the way, even dipping its tongue in a little cocoa dust and coriander seed. Pure fruit, deft daintiness of touch, cool, ripe, proudly Australian.

3   2006 Shiraz, Twins, Maverick Wines, Barossa Valley, South Australia, 14.5% ABV
   ◆ Lea and Sandeman, £11.95

Rich, full-frontal Aussie Shiraz is actually one of my favourite wine styles, but only when it's made with truly ripe – not *over*ripe – grapes from a good vineyard site, where the grapes' flavours increase as they linger on the vine rather than merely raisin in the sun's blaze. And the winemakers must have a vision of flavour, not just a desire to knock your socks off. This winery is called Maverick, i.e. they don't follow the common herd and sit there waiting for their grapes to turn to wizened currants on the vine. They pick them when they're ripe but still full of vitality. Old-timers will tell you that the Shiraz in Barossa can go from ripe to overripe in less than a day, between breakfast and tea. Luckily the mavericks listen to the old-timers. This wine is inspired. It's deep and dense, but achieves a thrilling balance between richness and freshness. The grapes have clearly revelled in the heat, but come in for tea when their mum calls, so what you get is a wine you can luxuriate in – black treacle and burnt black jelly on a jam tart, dark but not black chocolate, the softness of brioche, the freshness of the morning sky, the expression of a special place, as told by the Maverick.

4   2007 Rías Baixas, O Rosal, Bodegas Terras Gauda, Galicia, Spain, 12.5% ABV
◊ Les Caves de Pyrène, £12.25

They say that Rías Baixas, in the rainy, windy north-west corner of Iberia, is Spain's best white. And this Rías Baixas is the best example I've ever tasted. Does that mean this is…? Well, maybe it does. In general I find Rías Baixas to be good, dry, lemony stuff, sometimes softened with savoury cream, sometimes lightly washed with the iodine of the crashing waves nearby. But Terras Gauda take things on to a different level. One reason is that they don't just use the local Albariño grape, good though it is. They also grow the scented Loureiro and the virtually unheard of but brilliant Caiño Branco, which intensifies both the acidity and the richness of the final wine. I don't know anyone else who uses Caiño: they should start right away, because this memorable, prickly wine gives the most wonderful impression of grapefruit pith, apple core, lemon zest and rocks being magimixed into a kind of celestial froth. And when the excitement of the first mouthful fades, a most magical perfume spreads across your palate of fresh leather rubbed and soothed with floral

soap, of apricot skins and white peach flesh and the juice of a William pear dripping lazily down your chin onto your favourite tie.

5   2006 Soave Classico, Calvarino, Pieropan, Veneto, Italy, 12.5% ABV
◊ Bennetts, Liberty Wines, Valvona & Crolla, £15.99

Now, tell me, when was the last time you drank Soave of any sort, let alone paid white Burgundy money for it? Your silence is deafening me. And for the general run of the Soave mill, I'm not surprised. Like its near neighbour Valpolicella, Soave became far too popular, far too famous, and as the world's thirst grew, quality dropped to the floor. But real, true Soave, from the lovely hillside vineyards hidden up the valleys away from the stifling over-fertile plain, is one of Europe's most lovely white wines. Pieropan was the first of the modern era to attempt to revive Soave's ancient quality, and the Calvarino vineyard was the first for generations to be sold as a single-vineyard wine. It's a wonderful site, lovingly tended, producing wine of amazing purity and fascinating unexpected flavours. For a start it boasts an appetizing, mouthwatering aroma of fresh Kent Goldings hops. That's rare enough in beer, let alone wine. This mingles with the heady scent of unsmoked Havana tobacco leaf and cedar, but the fruit does fight back – fluffy white apple flesh and crisp green melon scented with the citrous perfume of boiled lemons – and all these aromas are wrapped together in crème fraîche and beeswax. That's what you pay the money for.

6   2007 Semillon, Tim Adams, Clare Valley, South Australia, 13% ABV
◊ Australian Wine Centre, Tesco, £9.20

Come the hour, come the man. My choice of favourite wines just wouldn't seem right without the latest vintage of Tim Adams' Semillon. And talk about not gouging on price. I looked back to my tastings of five years ago – the 2002 wine was magnificent, and it cost £8.99. A 21p increase in five years – the tax has gone up more than that. And not only is Tim's new vintage something I relish every year, but each release is different, in the way that wines are supposed to reflect the conditions of the harvest, but frequently don't nowadays. Last year his 2005 Semillon was rich and exotic, humming with the industry of bees lapping nectar. This year the 2007 is a bright, joyful thing of beauty. It is scented with nectarine and apple leaf dabbed with confectioner's cream. And the flavour is lush and soft, the nectarine joined by cling peach, brazil nuts and blood orange acidity sprinkled with kitchen spice and cinnamon custard. Delicious now, it'll grow waxy and honeyed over the years.

7 **2007 Sauvignon Blanc, Garuma Vineyard, Viña Leyda, Leyda Valley, Chile, 13.5% ABV**
◊ The Wine Society, £7.50

Up and down the Chilean coast there are numerous places where it's really cool and where Sauvignon can ripen slowly to the tongue-tingling crackling fruitiness that is its hallmark. This wine comes from a marvellous new area called Leyda. I've stood in this vineyard and gazed at the icy Pacific Ocean within shouting distance to the west. The wine's colour is water white. It's so fresh you can feel the prickle in your nose as you pick it up to smell. Taste it, and the spritzy prickle teases your tongue as the shock of the raw capsicum and nettle, lime zest, gooseberry and coffee bean dives into the tired recesses of your spirit and rips away the cobwebs and fatigue. Exemplary stuff.

8 **2006 Riesling, Grand Cru Eichberg, Philippe Zinck, Alsace, France, 12.5% ABV**
◊ Majestic Wine, £11.99

Nearly all the best dry Rieslings I come across nowadays are from the New World. Yet it's Alsace, on the German border in north-east France, that first made dry Riesling of world-class quality. The trouble is Alsace bottles look German, the labels sound German and, since we're not exactly in a pro-German wine national mood at the moment, we don't drink Alsace Riesling. Actually, this isn't new. Even when German wines were popular in the UK, Alsace wines were chiefly famous as the ones the wine trade loved to drink, but couldn't sell. And not being popular or trendy means prices have stayed fair. This is a beautiful wine from a tip-top vineyard, the Eichberg in Eguisheim, 900 years old and the driest microclimate in the area. It certainly imparts very individual flavours, with the appetizing sourness of a Bramley apple and the scratch of lime zest, rounded out with fresh greengage and ripe apple flesh fruit and a lingering aftertaste of dusty honey and ginger.

9 **2006 Tempranillo Reserve, Tim Adams, Clare Valley, South Australia, 13% ABV**
  ◆ Australian Wine Centre, £16.00

Tim Adams has been threatening the world with this beauty for several years now. He'll ambush you at wine tastings and persuade you to follow him for a taste of his new baby. He's a very big man with a very big hand- or, rather, fist-shake: he says follow, you follow. And each time I've seen his experimental Tempranillos, I've said, 'Wow, when can we get some?'. Well here it is. Tempranillo is one of the fastest-growing new varieties in Australia and it's clearly brilliantly suited to the coolish but sunny Clare Valley conditions. Tim has produced a wine that should be the role model for Tempranillo in Australia: its lovely dark fruit of scented loganberry and sweet sloes is brightened up with lime blossom and eucalyptus perfume and all of these flavours run right through the glyceriney and attractively tannic heart of the wine. Lovely now, it'll age beautifully.

10 **2005 Grüner Veltliner, Langenloiser Berg Vogelsang, Weingut Bründlmayer, Kamptal, Austria, 12.5% ABV**
  ◇ Waitrose, £12.99

Bründlmayer is such a star. Whatever the vintage conditions, he always produces quintessential wines, bursting with the personality of the grape variety and his carefully tended vineyard sites. 2005 wasn't nearly so easy a vintage in Austria as in many parts of Europe, and the low alcohol of 12.5% demonstrates that, but Bründlmayer has turned that to his advantage, producing a slightly prickly wine of brilliant originality. It manages to blend a dry rocky gauntness with the softness of brioche and the scent of honey and an amazing ripe winter vegetable flavour like white pepper mixed with uncooked turnip flesh. It may sound strange, but it's the essence of Grüner Veltliner, and it's delicious.

11 2005 Coteaux du Languedoc, Terrasses du Larzac, Mas des Brousses, Languedoc, France, 13% ABV

● Stone, Sun & Vine, £11.50

This is the south of France at its pleasure-brimming best. Most of the vast Midi zone down by the Med still takes its grapes to the local co-operative, where anything can happen to them, good or bad (mostly bad-ish). But every year more people, usually young couples, strike out on their own. At Mas des Brousses most of the grapes still go to the co-op because their own tiny cellar next to the church can't cope with the whole crop. Yet they keep back their best grapes and make a surprisingly cool-climate beauty: deep, savoury chocolate, damson skins and blackberry and toast, it displays a marvellous cool texture from a warm place. The label says 'fero tibi vinum dulce' – I bring you sweet wine. You sure do.

12 2004 La Grola, IGT Veronese, Allegrini, Veneto, Italy, 13.5% ABV

● The Wine Society, £13.50

If you want to find out just how good the wines of Valpolicella could be if they came from the classic, historic Valpolicella vineyards up in the Veronese hills, rather than the super-fertile sultry valley floor where most of the grapes are now grown, Allegrini is a must-buy producer for you. They don't try to internationalize their wines with Cabernet and Shiraz and God knows what, they simply maximize the great qualities of the local grapes. La Grola is a single vineyard, 300 metres up the hillside and would be accorded Grand Cru status under any French system. The core characteristic of true Valpolicella is the ability to offer lush fruit yet retain a cherry kernel, black chocolate bitterness. La Grola does that brilliantly: black chocolate and bitter almond seem to seesaw with cherry sauce and milk chocolate sweetness, cut through with the acid rub of peach skins. The balance between bitterness, sweetness and acid changes with every mouthful.

13 2006 Shiraz, Directors' Cut, Heartland Wines, Langhorne Creek-Limestone Coast, South Australia, 14.5% ABV
♦ Great Western Wine, £14.95

When this first appeared a few years back it was astonishing stuff, reeking of lime zest and eucalyptus ripping through blackcurrant fruit of almost painful intensity. That was when most of the fruit came from a new vineyard called Wirrega, in the middle of nowhere except eucalyptus forest. Now, most of the fruit comes from Langhorne Creek, just south of McLaren Vale, and the character has changed. That blast of lime and eucalyptus has given way to something much softer, lusher, more soothing in character. That's what Langhorne Creek is famous for – the ability to ripen grapes to a succulent concentration of richness without going troppo. This is a caressing mouthful of fudge and chocolate, vanilla and coconut cream all draped around a fine sweet core of ripe black plum and brazil nuttiness.

14 2007 Sauvignon Blanc, Fryer's Cove, Bamboes Bay, South Africa, 14% ABV

◊ Stone, Sun & Vine, £10.25

I've stood among the Sauvignon vines at Fryer's Cove, 350 kilometres north of Cape Town, with the wild Atlantic rollers drumming in my ears and the gales whipping across my face. When they say it's a cold-climate vineyard, wind-burned me is here to say that they're not joking. And that's what gives the memorable tangy flavour to the wine. Sunshine to ripen the grapes, cold winds to sharpen the acidity. You get a real sense of a mineral rawness of wind-swept stones tumbling through the wine, and a cascade of green flavours — nettles and green pepper, Bramley apples, parsley and kiwi — topped off with coffee bean and a squirt of ugli fruit acidity.

15 2005 Abadia Retuerta, Selección Especial, Vino de la Tierra de Castilla y León, Spain, 14% ABV

● Bennetts, Liberty Wines, Noel Young, £15.99

This wine was thrillingly good when it first appeared a few years ago, then, as often happens with new wines and new areas, it seemed to lose its way and its focus for a few vintages, but now it's triumphantly back. The vineyards are right next to the great — and expensive — Ribera del Duero zone, which produces many of Spain's finest reds. This is good enough to be in there with them in the top bracket. It's a dense, serious red, but not so self-obsessed that you can't gain immense pleasure from it. At the moment it's smelling of mint and vanilla and tasting of sturdy black fruit and chocolate. Give it a year or two and the chocolate will become spicy and sweet and the dark fruit will transform into the scented juicy lushness of blackcurrant and blackberry.

16   2006 Cabernet-Merlot, Woodlands, Margaret River, Western Australia, 13% ABV

◆ Great Western Wine, £14.95

When I have to conduct comparative tastings — New World versus Old World — I often pit a good Bordeaux against a similarly priced, or cheaper, Cabernet-Merlot from Western Australia. And the Australian wine usually wins, not because it tastes Australian, but because it tastes how you hoped the Bordeaux would taste. The Margaret River has only had vines for about 40 years, but the site was chosen because of its climatic similarities to Bordeaux in a good year and its ability to produce restrained, elegant flavours amid the flood of brash Aussie bruisers. This proves the point brilliantly. With its fresh basil and thyme perfume, its blackcurrant fruit sharpened by apple acid and the tang of blackcurrant leaves and softened with pastry, this is lovely now. But it will gain depth and beauty over the next few years, without losing its orchard bark and summer earth freshness, and be ideal for calm, contemplative aging.

17   2006 Sauvignon Blanc, Clifford Bay Reserve, Villa Maria, Marlborough, New Zealand, 14% ABV

◊ Oddbins, £14.99

Ah, Sauvignon lovers, step forward and be counted. If you love the crackle, the tang, the gorgeous unbridled, shouting, careering excitement of a wine that makes your tonsils wobble with its self-confidence and aggression, then this is for you. Yet when I say 'aggressive', the wine isn't raw or unfriendly, it's just unashamedly itself — packed with intense gooseberry, tomato leaf and blackcurrant leaf tanginess, scented with coffee beans, nettles and lime, yet delightfully deep in texture while being brilliantly bright and green. It stands proudly and says to the rest of New Zealand — hey, what's wrong with you guys, this is what Sauvignon should taste like.

18 **2005 Grenache, Fifth Wave, Langmeil, Barossa Valley, South Australia, 16% ABV**
◆ Oz Wines, £19.99

Barossa is famous for its ancient Shiraz vines, but the early settlers usually planted some Grenache as well, since that was a traditional blend in the southern Rhône Valley in France — it still is. Just a few really old Grenache vines have survived. Langmeil already have some of the oldest Shiraz vines I've ever seen, and

these Grenache were planted in the 1850s. They make small amounts of wonderful wine. This is rich in a completely different way to Shiraz, and copes with its high alcohol better. The baked strawberry jam is slightly burnt at the edge and daubed with honey, the scent is a jumble of mint and thyme and anis, while the texture mixes the jam with mint toffee and boulders. Thundering, wagon-wheeling wine.

19 **2006 Chardonnay (unfiltered), Saintsbury, Carneros, California, USA, 13.5% ABV**
◊ Majestic Wine, £15.99

Saintsbury was one of California's first truly modern wineries, started by a couple of guys I still call Mr Dick and Doctor Dave. I could use their surnames, but they've never really grown up enough to demand it. They've also never grown up enough to be swayed by fashion and marketeers into making the thick, wodgy Chardonnays that some opinion-formers would have us believe the wine-drinker wants. They understand their vines, their region, and what they like to drink themselves. So this is what they offer us: smooth, balanced, almost waxy texture, bright melon and pear fruit enriched just a bit with pineapple and given an appetizing savouriness with toasted hazelnuts and oatmeal.

20   **2005 Shiraz, The Aberfeldy, Tim Adams, Clare Valley, South Australia, 14.5% ABV**

♦ Australian Wine Centre, Tesco, £25.99

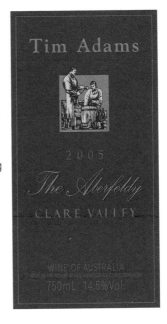

The vines at Aberfeldy were planted in 1904. I have to take my hat off to Tesco for offering us the chance of buying something that's made from vines planted only a couple of years after Queen Victoria died. The wine is made by Tim Adams, the guy who has probably been this guide's most consistent high-quality contributor over the years. I'm shutting my eyes and concentrating – no, I can't remember *ever* tasting a bad wine from this guy. And he has a very sensitive winemaking touch, which is crucial with such venerable vines – he draws out their essence rather than imposes his opinions. The essence is of rich plum, sweet red cherry, rosehips and spring blossom, a lush softness in a protective frame created by balance not fury, the creaminess of brazil nut flesh, the lick of Belgian milk chocolate, the wafting scent of toast. All the mellow beauty of old-vine Shiraz with none of the arrogant brutality that often nowadays accompanies it.

21   **2006 Cabernet Sauvignon-Merlot, Moda, Joseph, Primo Estate, McLaren Vale, South Australia, 15% ABV**

♦ Australian Wine Centre, £19.99

What I really should do is to ring up Joe Grilli, the wizard who makes Moda and say – look, if you gave me a range of your wines going back 10 years and more, I suspect they could hog the number one slot. Because this Moda is magnificent stuff, but it needs age. It's made like Italian Amarone, using dried grapes, second fermentation and a whole range of Italian dark arts – but, hey, Joe's Italian, the dark arts are second nature

to him. The result is fabulous, off-beam, black-hearted red that will be a world-beater at 10–15 years old. No merchant is going to hold the wine for 10 years: it's up to you. So, here's my tasting note for now. Impressive stuff, so dense and dark it's difficult to see through the shroud of tannin and extraction, but I see an almost toasted chocolate splashed with cocoa beans, fresh roasted Kenya coffee, blackberry and black rosa plum fruit heading towards prune, and a brazil nut flesh softness shadow-boxing with burly, grainy tannin. In 10 years' time, who knows what it will taste like, but I know it will be brilliant.

22 2005 Carso, Teran, Zidarich, Friuli-Venezia Giulia, Italy, 11.5% ABV
♦ Les Caves de Pyrene, £20.60

Hmm ... 20 quid. That's a lot of money to pay for a journey into the unknown. Because that's what you have here – flavours that you are unlikely to have come across before. To be honest, I shouldn't be surprised about the wild, unexpected flavours: these vineyards are way up in the no-man's land of north-east Italy, crunched in against Slovenia. And this brilliant red doesn't really owe its character to either country: it's a stunning original. It starts with a trumpet blast of red peppers, cherry tomato, cherry, graphite – and tannin. Surely, too much tannin? Well, hold the wine in your mouth. Tannin usually gets worse, not better. This tannin unbelievably fades to a lovely, rich, soft finish as a host of gentle flavours emerge: cocoa powder, coriander seed, apple purée and custard and that grand overweening scent of graphite demanding a little respect.

23 2004 Shiraz, Sanguine Estate, Heathcote, Victoria, Australia, 14.5% ABV
♦ Great Western Wine, £18.95

This is well-named: Sanguine. Although it doesn't exactly mean bloody – it could mean taking a calm, unflustered view of things – I prefer to think of the French for blood, *sang*, as I contemplate this wine, because the soils that grow it are the reddest I've ever visited. They stain everything in sight: even the sheep are red at Heathcote. These are some of Australia's most ancient soils – 500 million years and counting – and they produce a unique style of Shiraz quite unlike any others I know, their amazing lush texture accompanied by gorgeous fruit that never goes OTT. This has a perfume like polished cowboy boots and lovage and curry plant, and a flavour of ripe rosa plums, apple sauce and prunes, restrained yet yummy chocolate and toffee syrup all draped in the sticky scent of eucalyptus oil.

24   2003 Rioja Reserva, Contino, Spain, 13.5% ABV
♦ Marks & Spencer, £22.00

This is a delightful rarity: single-vineyard Rioja. Most Rioja is a blend of grapes and wine from different villages, by merchants who then sell it under a brand name. But this is from one high-class vineyard in the excellent Alavesa region. It has soothing, suave, ripe red fruit, mellowed by a touch of raisin ripeness and the warm, brown, clubman's drawing room scent of good oak, and is enlivened by a lime-zesty streak. Fuller than old-style Rioja, but less chunky than New Wave examples.

25   2005 Cabernet, Tim Adams, Clare Valley, South Australia, 14.5% ABV
♦ Australian Wine Centre, £11.00

Serious, balanced, rich Cabernet, marvellously dense, a perfect example of why Clare is such a special growing environment: the sun has ripened the grapes to their max, but the cool conditions have preserved a mouthwatering freshness. It still needs a few years' age, but if you like your reds thick and strong you can lay into it now. The mixture of leaf and blackcurrant in its smell is Bordeaux-like, and the dark blackcurrant fruit, lightened by mint yet hemmed in by tannin and acidity, is reminiscent of a young Pauillac. If that's not high praise, I don't know what is.

26 2002 Cornas, Grandes Bastides, Tardieu Laurent, Rhône Valley, France, 12.5% ABV
♦ Raeburn Fine Wines, £20.99

I can always rely upon Raeburn (see page 181) to come up with some really interesting wines. Here they've found a parcel of mature wine from the small Rhône village of Cornas – not easy to do, but the 2002 vintage wasn't popular, so if you sniff about you can get lucky. This Cornas is still fairly youthful, and has a lovely cool scent of flowers in bloom, blackberries and perfumed black chocolate. There's some appetizing tannin and acid to point up the flavours and a hint of stewed celery to sharpen your palate. A delightful, dry expression of cool-climate Syrah, and it's only 12.5% alcohol – just right.

27 2006 Graves, Berry's Own Selection, Extra Ordinary White, Bordeaux, France, 12.5% ABV
◊ Berry Bros & Rudd, £11.50

White Bordeaux can be one of France's greatest white wines, but few people seem to be aware of the fact, and merchants say it's really difficult to sell. This example is made by *red* wine supremo Jean-Michel Cazes of Château Lynch-Bages fame, but he's always had a soft spot for white and understands how to coax the best from his grapes. He's drawn out a mouthwatering nectarine and white peach fruit flavour with quite incisive passion fruit acidity and gentle, slightly singed custard richness that is an absolute delight, and which will age 3 or 4 years if you want it to.

28 2005 Shiraz, Hazyblur Wines, Adelaide Plains, South Australia, 14.9% ABV
♦ Oz Wines, £11.99

The Adelaide Plains is a torrid, baking, flat, exhausting place, and it was traditionally regarded as a pretty rubbish place to grow grapes, until the inspired Joe Grilli at Primo Estate proved that if you cared enough, you could produce exciting stuff there. Hazyblur obviously took note, because this Shiraz is a beauty, and it isn't *anything* like the Barossa beasts a short drive to the north. It's got a surprisingly fresh aroma of mint and violet, plum and toffee cream, and a flavour that gets darker and richer – blackcurrant mixes with the mint, and coconut and tarry toffee fight with eucalyptus and lime. Unusual, excellent.

+ Hazyblur also do a fine McLaren Vale Shiraz (£15.99): floral, black-fruited and shot through with ironstone.

29   2006 Gringet, Les Alpes, Vin de Savoie, D & P Belluard, Savoie, France, 12% ABV
◊ Les Caves de Pyrene, £12.90

What is Gringet? Well, some people say it's the same as Savagnin, a grape that makes earth-shattering wines a bit north of Savoie in the Jura mountains. Others say it's only related to Savagnin and, since a teetotal bishop can be first cousin to a drug-crazed rock'n'roller, I'll admit that the formidable Savagnin could be related to the delicious and not at all daunting Gringet. Even so, this isn't mainstream: Savoie rarely is. It's a full gold colour, speckled with high country mineral dust and tasting of cracked black pepper, spring greens and celery, but above all of overripe goldengages, nut syrup and spice and baked apple flesh going mushy inside its crinkly skin.

30   2005 Pinot Noir, Kooyong Estate, Mornington Peninsula, Victoria, Australia, 13.5% ABV
◆ Great Western Wine, £19.60

Pinot Noir likes cool conditions, but the first grape growers on the Mornington Peninsula, south of Melbourne, were so keen to prove that Australia could do cold that half the time the grapes never ripened and the wines were thin and mean.

hazyblur
2005 South Australia
Adelaide Plains Shiraz

Kooyong is just a bit warmer – just a little, nothing dramatic, but crucially the extra degree of warmth means that the Pinot is still elegant and restrained, but it *is* ripe. This has a gentle, mature, calm quality, far removed from the elbowing and shoving of much modern Australian wine, and is almost Burgundian in style – mellow, cherry-fruited, nuttily soft, showing a little grainy tannin, but with that mixture of red fruit glycerine softness and savoury scent that you can usually only find in places like Beaune. Well, you can find it here too.

31 2004 Cabernet Sauvignon, Sandalford Wines, Margaret River, Western Australia, 14.5% ABV
♦ Oz Wines, £11.99

An important Western Australian producer who made a big quality leap at the beginning of the century, and is still forging ahead. Western Australia's Margaret River prides itself on being able to create Bordeaux-like flavours – and it can, but with more fruit intensity and at a lower price. This has a lovely, suckable, blackcurrant pastille sweetness and a delicate violet scent, yet also carries its share of gritty pepper and a dry savoury finish. It *is* Bordeaux in style, but with the big plus of Australian quality fruit.

32 2006 Shiraz, Bishop, Glaetzer Wines, Barossa Valley, South Australia, 14.5% ABV
♦ Great Western Wine, £18.95

Ben Glaetzer named this wine after his mum. Not that his mum was a bishop; anything but. The fruit is from the Ebenezer vineyard, one of Barossa's top sites, though some of the wines from Ebenezer can be a bit over the top. This one gets it just right. It's not porty, but it *is* rich: mint and blackberry and blackcurrant get sloshed about with plum jam on buttered toast, prunes, leather and herbs. It's a big old thing, but there's beauty there as well as size.

33 2005 Barbera d'Alba, Josetta Saffirio, Piedmont, Italy, 13.5% ABV
   ◆ Corney & Barrow, £13.99

Well, if Italian wine is intent upon making itself more user-friendly, this Barbera is a pretty good standard bearer. It's a dense red colour, but the flavour isn't at all aggressive. What about rich red fruit that is mostly cranberries and redcurrants? What about scented fudge, tiramisu, vanilla pods and crème caramel topped off with buttered brazils? Cut through that with some gentle tannin and sprinkle a dusting of spice, and this is Italy with its glad-rags on – almost.

34 2006 Greco di Tufo, Feudi di San Gregorio, Campania, Italy, 13% ABV
   ◇ Booths, £11.99

Italy may be more famous for reds, but it does whites remarkably well, especially when it uses its indigenous grape varieties. Greco di Tufo is a southern variety capable of keeping its fresh, juicy profile under quite challenging sunny conditions in the hills behind Naples. It produces delightful stuff: a spicy aroma of pear flesh and peach and an almost lush but bright flavour of leather polished with beeswax, mint leaves thrown into the fruit salad of pear and peach, and the distant dry rub of stones.

35 2004 Coyam (organic), Viñedos Emiliana, Colchagua Valley, Chile, 14.5% ABV
   ◆ Tanners, £12.40

Chile has a rapidly growing band of young winemakers with the talent and vision to turn its stupendous grapes into great wine. But Alvaro Espinoza has been a young Turk for as long as Chile has been demanding a place in the international market, and he shows no signs of complacent middle age setting in just yet. Coyam is the result of a prodigious organic programme – beautiful vineyards producing exceptional grapes. It's deep stuff: dark, black, rich. Ideally you'd leave this 5–8 years to reach its peak. Well, do so if you can, but if not, you'll find a powerhouse here of black plum and blackcurrant, coal dust and smoke, cream, chocolate and toffee; impressive now, more beautiful in a few years.

36   2006 Chablis Premier Cru Beauroy, Domaine Jean-Marie Naulin, Burgundy, France, 13% ABV
◊ Fingal-Rock, £12.50

If you want wines naked as God intended, no make-up, no folderol, no fancy-dan winemaking, then Fingal-Rock is probably the wine merchant for you (see page 167 for details). This is fine Chablis exactly as it should be, mixing honeysuckle scent with gentle cooked apple fruit that hints at the softness of crumble pastry to come, and a mineral core as plain and unadorned as the soft limestone soils where the grapes grew.

37   2005 Ribera del Duero, Roble (organic), Dominio Basconcillos, Castilla y León, Spain, 14.5% ABV ◆ Vintage Roots, £9.99

A lot of Ribera del Duero spends too long in barrel – which is bonkers, because the fruit and personality are so good, why flatten them with the creamy embrace of too much new oak? This wine had just four months in barrel and is all the better for it. The ripe blackberry fruit sings out, the outdoor scents of mint and eucalyptus and thyme reach into every recess of the wine's mellow soft black heart, and the dusting of chocolate powder, cinnamon and clove is delightful seasoning rather than broad brash brutality.

38 2006 Riesling Kabinett, Ürziger Würzgarten, Dr Loosen, Mosel, Germany, 8% ABV
◊ Waitrose, £11.99

Beautiful classic gentle Mosel wine, spectacularly fresh, soothingly soft and very low in alcohol. Riesling can reach a heavenly flavour ripeness while holding on to its springtime freshness and, by leaving a little unfermented sugar in the wine, flavours of crystalline purity and balance can be created. Würzgarten means 'spice garden': it's the name of a precious little suntrap of a vineyard in this cold region. In the hands of Ernst Loosen, the grapes are transformed into a delicate soufflé of honey and sugar-puffs poured over a bed of slate, brioche dough and Cornish ice cream, cut with boiled lemon zest and wrapped in apple peel and spice.

39 2006 Syrah, TMV Tulbagh Mountain Vineyards, Swartland, South Africa, 14% ABV
● Waitrose, £12.99

TMV are a new force in South African wine, aware of what is going on in places like Australia and the Rhône Valley in France, and intending to use such experience to maximize the potential of the Cape. This is fine Syrah – or Shiraz – in anyone's money. It's very deep, but not coarse or overripened. The tannin is evident but acts as a caution to the richness of blackberry, plum, milk chocolate and cocoa powder. And when you've swallowed the wine, there's an alluring flavour of fresh Jersey cream left lingering on your tongue.

40 1990 Vouvray, Aigle Blanc, Prince Poniatowski, Loire Valley, France, 12% ABV
◊ Waterloo Wine, £11.00

I couldn't resist putting this one in. I don't know where they find stuff like this, but Waterloo (see page 188) is one of those inspiring wine companies that can always be relied upon to excite and amaze. This is *not* a modern wine. It affords me a mellow sense of Laurie Lee childhood, hay bales and shady barns, bread dough and fresh-cropped honey mixed with the Bramley apple peel from a pie, daubed with quince jelly and medlar fruit. And somewhere in the heart of the wine, the old country stones bake in the lazy summer sun.

100 FOR AROUND A TENNER

When I look back over the last few years at the kind of wines that I would be most likely to open with supper, with Sunday lunch, when friends drop by to watch the football, it's the £7 to £10 arena that gets raided most often. This is an area where there should be enough leeway for everyone – producer, shipper, retailer – to make a decent profit. To be honest, when I'm keen for a good glass of something refreshing, interesting, satisfying, this under-a-tenner world is my playing field. Funnily enough £7.99, which should be an excellent price level to find all kinds of interesting wines, has been sadly abused by the buy-one-get-one-free mob – the bogof hooligans who artificially inflate a wine price so that they can then seem to offer a stunning bargain to the unwary shopper. Does anyone really think Hardy's Crest or Gallo's basics are worth £7.99? Please! They're worth four quid and – surprise, surprise – that's what the discount brings them down to. Sadly, it means that for wines that really are worth £7.99, far too many shoppers simply wait for the deep discount to kick in, and so don't buy the wine. Well, in this selection, the £7, £8, £9 and £10 wines are worth the full price, and we should pay it.

- I've divided this section into whites followed by reds, kicking off with wines at the top end of this price bracket.

- Rosé wines have their own section on pages 102–107.

WHITE WINE

2006 Chardonnay, Special Cuvée, Montes Alpha, Casablanca Valley, Chile, 14% ABV
Majestic, Morrisons, Tesco, £10.99

Aurelio Montes, the Chilean star who makes this wine, doesn't like it when I tell him how good his whites are looking. Reds are his obsession. But he does make awfully good whites. This is exactly the style of Chardonnay that Chile does so well, with a spicy, pineappley smell and a dry, sensuous, scented texture of nectarines and soft oak that manages to be fresh and balanced, but round and warming at the same time.

2005 Marsanne, Tahbilk, Victoria, Australia, 13.5% ABV
Wine Rack, £10.49 (3 for 2, £6.99)

Marsanne is an excellent Rhône Valley white grape – or should I say golden grape, because you don't often see it unblended, but when you do it's usually golden. This is from the lakes of Central Victoria in Australia: it's a lovely, fat, squashy autumnal mix of licorice and quince jelly, honey and boiled lemons all wrapped in a golden shroud.

2007 Semillon, Brokenwood, Hunter Valley, New South Wales, Australia, 11.5% ABV
Flying Corkscrew, Liberty Wines, Villeneuve Wines, £10.49

This is fascinating wine. The Hunter Valley is such a paradoxical place. It's virtually sub-tropical, a couple of hours' drive north of Sydney. When the sun shines, the grapes bake. When the rains fall, the vines drown. But somehow the Semillon seems to thrive in these insane conditions, and produces world-class wine at very low alcohol levels. This has the character of cool running right through it – cool greengage skins, cool white-fleshed apple and peach, cool orange juice and lemon zest, dust and stones – and then,

right at the end, a suggestion of tobacco and the merest hint of honeyed raisins to remind you it does get very hot in the Hunter, even if the storms force them to pick when the grapes are still virtually green.

2007 Pecorino, Terre di Chieti, Colle dei Venti, Caldora, Abruzzo, Italy, 13% ABV
Wine Rack, £9.99 (3 for 2, £6.66)

I know, I know. I heard all the jokes the first time I used this at a tasting. Well, keep laughing, but try the wine too, because that'll keep you smiling long after the punchline. One thing it doesn't taste of is cheese. It does the sort of palate-cleansing, chilled aperitif job that Sauvignon is so good at, or Australian Riesling. It has a most attractive high lemon pith acidity, good mineral dusty dryness, ripe apple fruit and a scent somewhere between fresh leather and lavender.

2007 Sauvignon Blanc, Boreham Wood Single Vineyard, Clark Estate, Awatere Valley, Marlborough, New Zealand, 13.5% ABV
Flagship Wines, £9.99

There is a trend for New Zealand Sauvignons to become fatter, sweeter and definitely less crunchy and green. Hopefully the old saying 'if it ain't broken don't fix it' will resurface in the noddles of the Kiwi winemakers before South Africans and Chileans decide that they'll take up the cudgels for the crunchy and green. But one area of Marlborough still believes in green: Awatere – it's further south, colder, but quite big enough to supply most of our needs. If you like gooseberries and green apple, green pepper, nettle and lemon zest all wrapped in a lovely mouthwatering texture, then look for Awatere in the small print.

2007 Sauvignon Blanc, Vision, Cono Sur, Casablanca Valley, Chile, 13% ABV
Threshers, Wine Rack, £9.99 (3 for 2, £6.66)

If I had to taste this among a bunch of New Zealand Sauvignons, I'm not sure I could tell it apart. The Cono Sur winery in Chile uses cool-climate Casablanca Valley grapes and produces a lovely wine that is quite soft, yet has lots of green leafy flavours – nettle, blackcurrant leaf, green apples, green pepper and lemon zest.

2007 Grüner Veltliner, Wachtberg, Salomon Undhof, Kremstal, Austria, 12.5% ABV
Lea and Sandeman, £9.95

Ah, Grüner Veltliner. I'd strongly advise you to start learning how to pronounce the name because, as we become tired of superripe New World flavours and fatigued by excess alcohol in our wines, Austria's cool-climate Grüner Veltliner is a beacon of hope. It is a brilliant grape because, underripe or fully ripe, it offers fabulously refreshing and satisfying flavours, and it often performs best at around 12.5% alcohol. White pepper is one of its marker tastes, and this has it, along with anis and mint, tangy grapefruit zest and apple flesh, and a double treat of spritzy tingle on your tongue and a sprinkling of Danube mineral dust.

2007 Semillon-Sauvignon Blanc, Harewood Estate, Great Southern, Western Australia, 13.5% ABV
Great Western Wine, £9.95

Western Australia has made such a success of the classic white Bordeaux blend that in blind tastings I regularly put them down as top Bordeaux. But I must learn, because actually they exhibit a zestier, leaner style, more lemon and green apple peel and coffee bean, pure and limpid, with a chill streak of stones cutting across the sharp, fresh fruit.

2006 Bordeaux Blanc, Château Le Grand Verdus, France, 12% ABV
Friarwood, £9.90

A good example of how the lesser-known châteaux of Bordeaux would be much better employed making tasty whites – and rosés for that matter – than struggling to create big dark reds from vineyards that aren't up to the job. White grapes ripen more easily than reds, and don't need such high alcohol levels to show at their best. This wine is only 12% – and is all the better for it. The fresh nettle and green pepper tang isn't overwhelmed by the attractively peachy fruit and can bond with the lemon zest and green apple peel acidity while balancing out a delightful texture of soft cream cheese.

2006 Silvaner Kabinett, Trocken, Würzburger Abtsleite, Juliusspital, Franken, Germany, 12.5% ABV
Savage Selection, £9.60

I've been seeing rather more Franken wines recently because my new next-door neighbour went to school in the top vineyard village of Iphofen. And their subtle charms are getting to me. There's nothing intense or head-turning about this wine – it's just a lovely, gentle drink. There is dry apple peel, dabbed with honey and splashed with the coolness of mountain water running over stones. Everything is mellow, minor key.

2006 Riesling Kabinett, Piesporter Goldtröpfchen, Weingut Kurt Hain, Mosel, Germany, 8% ABV
Tanners, £9.50

If you've ever gasped in horror at the abysmal quality of a Piesporter Michelsberg, banish the memory from your mind, because Michelsberg was a made-up name for a miserable made-up wine that had nothing to do with Piesport. Piesport is one of Germany's greatest wine villages, and Goldtröpfchen is its greatest vineyard. Goldtröpfchen means 'little golden drops' and is a heavenly crescent of vines on a beautiful bend above the Mosel river. This is one of its lighter offerings – some literally drip honey, they're so lush – but it still leaves a lovely trail of honey in your mouth as well as a bright grapiness, the acidity of green apple and the soft satisfaction of a fluffy apple turnover.

2006 Bacchus, Chapel Down, Kent, England, 11.5% ABV
Waitrose, £9.49

It's English fizz that has been getting all the attention recently, but it was ethereally light white wines that got the whole industry moving, long before they decided that the conditions in southern England were too similar to those of Champagne to ignore. The Bacchus is the grape that growers agree makes England's most characteristic dry white – well, almost dry: most English whites aren't totally dry, but they're dry enough. This one tastes as though someone had emptied a bottle of elderflower cordial into the vat and then stirred it with a sprig of hawthorn cut from a hedgerow. Some mild Muscat and a noticeable grapefruit acidity rounds off a classic English mouthful.

2007 Grüner Veltliner, Obere Steigen, Weingut Huber, Traisental, Austria, 12.5% ABV
Oddbins, £9.49

Grüner Veltliner is a marvellous Austrian grape, particularly when it's kept just this side of full ripeness, because its savoury greenness is its most appealing characteristic. This has it in spades; it's so bright and zippy it foams on your tongue as the flavours swirl about your mouth – sage and grapefruit, greengage skin and the skin of green figs, honeydew wildly paired with sausagemeat and the perfume of summer-warmed stones.

2007 Sauvignon Blanc, Origin, Grove Mill, Marlborough, New Zealand, 12.5% ABV
Wine Rack, £9.49 (3 for 2, £6.33)

Grove Mill pride themselves on getting to Carbon Neutral status before just about any other winery. This is good traditional Kiwi Sauvignon, the type that has made the style so popular in the UK. Coffee beans, green apples, green pepper, a flicker of nettles and kiwi fruit and a good dry scrape of riverbed stones – tangy and sharp, but no raw edges.

2007 Riesling, Tim Adams, Clare Valley, South Australia, 12% ABV
Australian Wine Centre, Tesco, £9.20

Brilliant summer white, garden party white, but is so good and interesting that seafood and South-East Asian cuisine will be panting for it during the rest of the year. It's such a pure flavour, crystalline lemon zest and cooking apple skin rolled in a cascade of bright dry pebbles. A hint of brioche and a suggestion of honey to come softens up its pithy, dry style without compromising its austerity.

2007 Chardonnay, Allandale, Hunter Valley, New South Wales, Australia, 13.5% ABV
Oz Wines, £8.99

Allandale makes one of the most scented and subtle Chardonnays in the Hunter Valley. Of course, scent and subtlety are not what you'd expect from a Hunter Chardie, so this is a delightful high-class oddball, almost floral in its aroma, the springtime blossom of peaches and apples mixed with the clean bright crispness of melon. The flavour is more summery, and the peach and melon fruit turns to gold as mild toasty spice and a mouth-watering acidity combine to create a texture I wish more Australians would try to emulate.

2006 Marsanne-Viognier, The Hermit Crab, d'Arenberg, McLaren Vale, South Australia, 13.5% ABV
Waitrose, £8.99

The McLaren Vale, south of Adelaide, specializes in grape varieties from France's southern Rhône Valley, and d'Arenberg specializes in palate-busters, red or white. So it comes as no surprise that this white Rhône blend simply oozes fat indulgent peach, quince and pineapple fruit – the pineapple almost tastes like those slices you'd get on Gammon Hawaii, a *very* long time ago. D'Arenberg don't do subtlety, so a leathery texture and the cat's-tongue rasp of peach skin seems perfectly natural.

2007 Riesling, Eldredge Vineyards, Clare Valley, South Australia, 12% ABV
Australian Wine Centre, £8.99

Clare Valley Rieslings can be very austere, almost harsh. And they can be over 13% alcohol. Eldredge is neither. It's only 12%, with all the attractive lightness of being that brings. And it's surprisingly mild and gentle, the citrus element more like lemon flower than lemon zest, the fruit more green apple flesh than peel, and though there is some mouthwatering lemon juice acidity, the core of the wine is as gentle as the cake mix for a Victoria sponge.

2007 Sauvignon Blanc, Goldwater, Marlborough, New Zealand, 13.5% ABV
Majestic Wine, £8.99

The Goldwaters make some of New Zealand's most traditional and serious red wines on Waiheke Island, out in the sounds off Auckland. But they saw the world going mad for Sauvignon and rightly reckoned Marlborough in the South Island was the best place to grow it. This is full-bodied but flooded with crackling green flavours: nettle and lime zest, green pepper and passionfruit. Green-scented, green-hearted wine.

2007 Sauvignon Blanc, Shepherds Ridge (Wither Hills), Marlborough, New Zealand, 13% ABV
Marks & Spencer, £8.99

Shepherds Ridge is made by the supremely trendy Wither Hills winery in Marlborough; the style is usually just a bit broader and fatter than Wither Hills' regular cuvée. But there's still loads of green there – mint leaf, nettles, green apple and lime zest – and anyway, some people like their Sauvignon just a little more full-bodied, without losing its tang.

2007 Viognier, Single Vineyard, Anakena, Rapel Valley, Chile, 13.5% ABV
Wine Rack, £8.99 (3 for 2, £5.99)

Viognier is a wine with so much potential apricot richness that sometimes it becomes just too fleshy and self-indulgent to enjoy. But when the balance is right, the wine is delicious. Anakena is a good outfit and this is from one of their best individual vineyards; Chilean fruit quality is, in any case, famous. Here, juicy apricot mixes with the cat's tongue rasp of apricot skins and refreshing acidity to create a rich, grand, unctuous but very drinkable mouth-filler.

2007 Viognier-Riesling-Chardonnay, Ona, Anakena, Rapel Valley, Chile, 13.5% ABV
Oddbins, £8.99

This is an intriguing mix. Three totally different varieties, all with strong personalities – can they marry? Well, yes they can. Chilean Viognier is powerful stuff and often needs a bit of cooling of its brow; Chilean Riesling is citrous and scented; and Chilean Chardonnay is plump and tropical. This ménage à trois pits apricot against grapefruit, peach syrup and pineapple against lime juice acidity and lemon zest: it makes for a very good, balanced, juicy, fruity tropical white.

Xavier, Vin de Table, France, 14% ABV Big Red Wine Company, £8.95

The producer isn't allowed to say which grape varieties he uses, nor where they are grown. He can't even put a vintage on the bottle because he's quite purposefully broken some stupid French wine laws to make the wine that *he* wanted to. So, I'd *guess* that this is a good example of old southern Rhône Valley white varieties performing very well in modern hands. It has a lovely peach blossom scent, a smell of pears and kitchen spice, and a bright, clear flavour of nectarines and white peach cut with peach skin acidity and rounded off with ginger and cinnamon spice.

2007 Sauvignon Blanc, Vergelegen, Stellenbosch, South Africa, 13.5% ABV Waitrose, £8.79

Andre Van Rensburg is a helluva winemaker, and his Sauvignon Blancs have led the way to the Cape being seen as one of the world's best producers. His vineyards are blasted by southerly winds hurtling in from the Antarctic, so you get sunshine and chill – perfect for Sauvignon. This is haughty, serious stuff, ripe with green pepper and nettles, ripely scented lemons, freshly roasted coffee beans, and the palate-scouring dryness of cold stones.

2006 Sauvignon Blanc, Matahiwi Estate, Wairarapa, New Zealand, 13% ABV
Oddbins, £8.49

Not all New Zealand Sauvignon comes from the famous Marlborough region. A small amount comes from Wairarapa, just over the mountains from Wellington in the North Island. This is a little softer than a typical Marlborough Sauvignon, but is still a very nice drop: coffee bean and green apple freshness, ripe, juicy, soft fruit and nippy lemon zest acidity. Attractive, elegant Kiwi Sauvignon.

2007 Sauvignon Blanc, Villa Maria/Waitrose, Marlborough, New Zealand, 13.5% ABV
Waitrose, £8.49

When a supermarket goes into cahoots with a supplier for a joint venture own label, you tend to think, OK, what corners are going to be cut here? But Waitrose were very wise in choosing Villa Maria, who understand both the top and the bottom of the market very well. They make one of the most reliable, best-selling Kiwi Sauvignons at around £8, but I think Waitrose's label is better – aggressive, leafy, lemon pith and zest, Bramley apple and gooseberry. It has loads of Sauvignon zip. My only criticism would be that with these excellent green flavours, couldn't they make it a touch drier?

2007 Sauvignon Blanc, Sandy Ridge, Seifried, Nelson, New Zealand, 12.5% ABV
The Oxford Wine Company, £8.40

Nelson is just over the hills from the more famous Marlborough region. It's a little warmer, and a little wetter, and the effect is a slightly gentler but still refreshing and tasty glass of Sauvignon. There's still passionfruit and lemon zip, some green leaf and kiwi, but the appearance of not quite dry peach flesh in the heart of the wine takes away some of the kick.

sandy
ridge

Nelson
New Zealand
2007

Sauvignon Blanc

2006 Riesling, Blue Slate, Dr Loosen, Mosel, Germany, 8% ABV
Somerfield (selected stores only), £8.19

Blue Slate is a reference to the vineyard composition on these vertiginous slopes overlooking the Mosel River. In a cold wet place like the Mosel Valley, the slopes need to be steep and warm to ripen the grapes, the slithery slate provides just the right conditions, and Ernst Loosen is a star winemaker, the ideal man for converting the fruit into light, low-alcohol but fantastically lively wine. By lively I mean the wine almost fizzes on your tongue, but the flavour is surprisingly, delightfully soft: cream and brioche dough and lemon cake mixed with honey – the lemon zest provides the necessary snap for this delicate beauty.

2007 Riesling, Extra Special (Knappstein), Clare Valley, South Australia, 13.5% ABV
Asda, £8.12

All the big supermarkets seem to have managed to source good Australian Rieslings. We now need to persuade you all to give them a try. Because although they're ideally suited to the current anti-oak movement in wine-drinking, a lot of people are still unhappy with the German name Riesllng as the foetid phantom of Liebfraumilch swims nauseously in front of their giddy eyes. Block out the old nightmare. Embrace the new reality. Australian Riesling is as dry and citrous a wine as you will find anywhere on this earth. This one isn't harsh, it's really quite soft, but it does have a gentle/sharp flavour of baked cooking apples and cooked lemons and dry peach flesh. I thought I could detect some Rose's West Indian lime marmalade and some fresh paint. Ripe soft fruit wrapped round with the citrous embrace of lemon pith.

2007 Furmint, Verus Vineyards, Ormoz, Slovenia, 12% ABV
The Real Wine Company, £7.99

If you can't speak Slovenian it's a bit difficult to work out what this wine is: the back label is all in Slovenian. Anyway, the winery's called Verus – though they've thoughtfully put the R back to front to confuse you further. So, if you get past all that, this is actually rather good. Slovenian wines in general are extremely good but, fellas, it's like with Greek wines – you do need to make it easier for us Brits to have the slightest idea what you're trying to sell. We might like it. We might buy it. Especially if it's like this – tangy, zesty, aggressive, refreshing, almost spritzy. It does the Sauvignon job of revitalizing the palate rather well.

2007 Sauvignon Blanc, Dashwood, Vavasour, Marlborough, New Zealand, 13.5% ABV
Oddbins, £7.99

This is one of my great stand-bys. I probably use this Sauvignon for more tastings during the year than any other. Why? Because it's green, aggressive, sharp yet ripe, mouthfilling yet mouthwatering. The bulk of its grapes come from the ultra-cool Awatere zone of Marlborough, and that gives it the green kick of gooseberry, lime, blackcurrant, tomato leaf and green apple that makes me salivate. The 2007 is a little fatter than usual, but not so's you'd notice.

2007 Sauvignon Blanc, De Grendel, Tijgerberg, Cape of Good Hope, South Africa, 13.5% ABV Oddbins, £7.99

This is a wonderful vineyard site. You clamber to the top of the Tijgerberg hill and the great arc of the Atlantic coast sweeps away to Cape Town right beneath you. The Atlantic's ice-cold here, and the wine is chilly, but the sun shines and this potent mix creates exciting Sauvignon: green with nettles, parsley and dill, licked by the tumbling rocks of the Tijgerberg, yet with a delightful creaminess and a whiff of smoke.

2007 Sauvignon Blanc, Limited Selection, Montes, Leyda Valley, Chile, 13.5% ABV
Majestic, £7.99

Leyda is an ice-cold but sunny area that is showing fantastic form with Sauvignon. This time, we're on the Chilean coast, radically cooled by Antarctic currents sweeping up from the south. The wine has a thrilling taut acidity, green and sharp but also full and ripe. Magic. It smells of tomato leaf and blackcurrant leaf and Bramley apples; in the mouth this confident youthful full-throttle thrust adds mint and green pepper, and ends with the crisp crunch of Bramley apple peel.

2007 Sauvignon Blanc, The Reach, Vavasour, Marlborough, New Zealand, 13% ABV
Tesco, £7.99

Too many New Zealand Sauvignons are becoming fat and sweaty and sweet. Not this one. The fruit comes from one of the Marlborough region's coolest corners and the flavour bursts with tangy greenness: tomato leaf, blackcurrant leaf, gooseberry, green pepper and lime, and even a hint of horseradish. If you like it tangy, your tonsils will shiver with delight when you swallow this.

2007 Sauvignon Blanc, Domaine Octavie, Touraine, Loire Valley, France, 12.5% ABV
Threshers, Wine Rack, £7.99 (3 for 2, £5.33)

Just when you thought you were going to find all your Sauvignon Blanc pleasure in the New World, along comes the cool 2007 summer in France, and suddenly the Loire Valley, which has been increasingly comatose recently, rebounds with bright, sprightly Sauvignons to tickle your tonsils. Domaine Octavie is a serious Touraine producer and this has slightly squashy green apple fruit – it's attractive, don't worry – and good coffee bean and nettle aroma: clean, simple, mouthwatering.

2007 Villa Antinori, Tuscany, Italy, 12% ABV
Morrisons, £7.99, Tanners, £7.70

They grow a lot of white grapes in Tuscany – they used to mix them with red to make insipid Chianti – which need to be turned into something tasty. Antinori's the man. Antinori is world famous for his red wines, but he's given a lot more attention to whites in the past few years and it shows. This wine is low in alcohol and has an intentional flicker of spritz on the tongue that goes with the crisp, juicy apple fruit, hint of honey and mild Virginia tobacco scent. And there's an attractively insistent acidity. I found myself wondering, would the peel of an ugli fruit taste like this?

2006 Viognier, Vent di Damo, Vin de Pays des Portes de Mediterranée, Les Terrasses d'Eole, Languedoc, France, 14% ABV
Adnams, £7.99

The label says that Vent di Damo – the name of the wine – refers to a wind that 'fluttered ladies' skirts. This glimpse of forbidden fruit…' yes, well, I could go on. But let's check out the wine. Ah, 'sensuous, lush, thick-lipped style' – those are my notes, so I'm obviously caught up in the whole palaver. 'Not blowsy, merely careless in her diet.' What? Dear oh dear. Anyway, it's a lovely rich wine, fleshy, full of ripe pear and apricot fruit. That should do. I need a cold shower.

2007 Greco, Le Ralle, Alovini, Basilicata, Italy, 13% ABV
Tanners, £7.95

Greco is a really good grape that it would be nice for us to see more of. Well, if we drank more of it, more wine merchants would go looking for an example, so it's up to us. The grape came from Greece originally (Greco? Geddit?) and is grown quite widely in Italy's south: it is greatly benefiting from the recent revolution in white winemaking there. This comes from the mountains of Basilicata, south of Naples, and mixes fluffy apple and dry peach flesh with a touch of nutty brioche softness, but not enough to take away from the wine's basic shiny mineral austerity.

2007 Verdicchio di Matelica, Colle Stefano, Marche, Italy, 13% ABV
Les Caves de Pyrene, £7.80

Most Verdicchio comes from the Castelli di Jesi area down towards the eastern Italian coast – and all that stuff that used to be sold in a bottle that looked like Marilyn Monroe after a week at a health farm came from down there. But the small area of Matelica, up in the hills towards Umbria, produces much more exciting wine, partly because its Verdicchio grape is a special local mutant of far greater ambition and originality than the collar-and-tie coastal variety. This is intensely appley – fat apple, rich stewed apple, scented apple – but waxy in texture until a tile of slate cuts through the ripeness with its keen, cold edge and your tongue is left pondering a mellow coolness almost touched by snow.

2007 Sauvignon Blanc, Explorers Vineyard, Marlborough, New Zealand, 12.5% ABV
Co-op, £7.75

The Co-op goes to one of Marlborough's top growers for this Sauvignon and it's always sharp, tangy and full of fruit. But it's never raw – the lime zest and green pepper, gooseberry and blackcurrant leaf vivacity is matched by sweet green apple flesh ripeness and a palate-cleansing scraping of fresh summer earth.

2007 Mâcon-Chardonnay, Adnams Selection White Burgundy, Cuvée Paul Talmard, Domaine Talmard, Burgundy, France, 13.5% ABV
Adnams, £7.50

If you thought Chardonnay was the name of a village in Australia, it isn't, it's a village in France! In southern Burgundy, to be exact, near the town of Mâcon. Since they grow almost nothing but Chardonnay in the area around there, it is reasonable to assume that this is where the mighty golden grape comes from. It certainly produces pretty nice stuff as Mâcon-Chardonnay – succulent honey and crunchy ripe apple given a Burgundian sheen of oatmeal and stones, with an aftertaste of marrow jam.

2006 Chardonnay, Private Bin, Villa Maria, East Coast, New Zealand, 13.5% ABV Somerfield, £7.49

In the rush for its Sauvignon Blanc, New Zealand's Chardonnay often gets forgotten. But the Kiwis make some of the world's best Chardonnay in many different styles. This comes from Gisborne, New Zealand's 'Chardonnay Capital'. It's warm, but quite wet, yet these slightly worrying conditions produce delightful gentle Chardonnay, with melon, pear and apple fruit, a touch of spice, bright fresh acidity – quite simply, everything a big-volume commercial Chardonnay should be.

2006 Gewürztraminer, Taste the Difference (Cave de Turckheim), Alsace, France, 13% ABV Sainsbury's, £6.99

I suppose it's an acquired taste, but I do like a good Gewürztraminer, and I feel it could become much more popular if we pretended it was less spicy and

exotic and irresistible than it really is. We should stand up to the puritan within us. I recommend you try this lush but dry mouthful of lavender and tea rose petals and polished waxed leather, with just a hint of Nivea creme and the make-up powder of a matinée actress slightly past her bloom.

2007 Sauvignon Blanc, Vina Tabali, Limarí Valley, Chile, 13.5% ABV Booths, £6.99

Chile is developing new cool-climate areas up and down its coast as fast as it can. Limarí is way north and you'd think it would be too hot for white grapes to thrive, but an icy wind whips through the vineyards every day and you get the magic conditions that made New Zealand Sauvignons famous – loads of sun to ripen everything fully, and chill winds to keep the freshness in the grapes. So the wine is biting and full-bodied at the same time – grapefruit and nettle, lime and rolling stones but nothing too raw to make your gums fret.

2007 Sauvignon Blanc, Reserva, Montes, Casablanca Valley, Chile, 13.5% ABV
Waitrose, £6.99, Majestic, £6.79

A few years ago you'd have said, Chilean Sauvignon – mild, dull stuff – forget it. New Zealand ruled. Everyone else also-ran. But that was a time when Chardonnay led the white wine world, and New Zealand was producing more than enough Sauvignon to cope. Well, now Sauvignon is top dog. Any country that has a lot of sun and chill winds to cool the vineyards should do well with Sauvignon, and Chile has just those conditions. The Casablanca Valley has damp fogs in the morning and icy coastal winds in the evening, which gives full, very dry wine, green apple fruit slashed with lemon zest and juice and the cold rumble of stones.

2006 Semillon, Denman Vineyard, Tesco Finest (McGuigan Simeon), Hunter Valley, New South Wales, Australia, 10.5% ABV Tesco, £6.99

Tesco has always offered a really good, true-to-life Semillon from the Denman Vineyard, a vast spread in the north of the Hunter Valley. Sometimes it positively pummels you with its personality, but this vintage is a little more restrained: it's only 10.5% alcohol, so that would help. But it still exhibits classic Hunter Semillon flavours of putty and lemon pith and the dust from a stone-crushing plant. Just the habitual custardy softness is lacking, but I'm sure that will arrive if you keep the wine for a year or two.

2007 Rolle, Vin de Pays des Coteaux de Murviel, Domaine de Coujan, Languedoc, France, 13% ABV Great Western Wines, £6.60

The old-time experts used to pooh-pooh white wines from France's Mediterranean coast. They weren't very polite about the reds. They were positively libellous about the whites. But there have been decent white grape varieties growing there for centuries, and modern winemaking methods mean we can now see the beauty of these neglected varieties. Rolle is one of the best of the old varieties, especially when grown on the chalk soils at Coujan, and this wine sucks up the lavender and

thyme from the surrounding hills and wraps them around delicious overripe Cox's apple and pear flesh fruit cut through with lemon zest and slashed by a seam of almost vindictive minerality.

2007 Côtes du Rhône, Domaine de la Bastide, Rhône Valley, France, 14% ABV Connolly's, £6.40

Single-estate Côtes du Rhône is one of the best ways to get top-quality French white for a very sensible price. These wines aren't much sought after yet, but they should be because, in a world that is tiring of heavy, overoaked whites, Rhône flavours are full and round but based on fruit, scent and herbs, not wood. This manages to be juicy *and* sappy, scented with peach blossom and dill, dripping with ripe pear and golden peach flesh and sharpened up with citrus zesty acid.

RED WINE

2005 Shiraz, Selkirk, Bremerton Wines, Langhorne Creek, South Australia, 15% ABV
Flagship Wines, £10.99

Langhorne Creek, south of Adelaide, has long been famous for growing fruit that gave lush, soft wines, but most of the fruit was blended away. Wolf Blass and Jacob's Creek wines became famous on the back of Langhorne fruit, yet very few properties in Langhorne made their own wine. This is changing as producers realize how popular these joyous, juicy reds can be under their own colours. A mouthful of this deep, scented red, dark with the juiciness of blackberry and plum and lush with the richness of chocolate tinged with the perfume of flowers will show you what I mean.

2006 Syrah, Apalta Vineyard, Montes Alpha, Colchagua Valley, Chile, 14.5% ABV
Tesco, Waitrose, £10.99

Apalta is a wonderful vineyard, a limestone crescent that faces away from the sun – but that's sometimes not a bad thing in Chile, where the sun shines virtually non-stop all summer. The grapes still ripen perfectly, but they don't bake. Here, you get the richness of black plums and blackberry, the sweetness of fudge and crème brûlée, but it isn't cloying: the black chocolate tannin keeps the richness in order, and the texture is really mouthwatering and tongue-cleansing.

2006 Brouilly, Château du Pavé, Beaujolais, France, 13% ABV
Christopher Piper, £10.35

This beauty from Beaujolais makes me wonder, for the hundredth time this year, why don't we drink more Beaujolais? It's never been better, and with its fresh bright fruit and lack of oak it could be such a crowd-pleaser. Maybe we still want Beaujolais to cost a fiver or less. Well, nearly all the Beaujolais I've recommended this year has been from single estates in top villages. They're boutique wines, and if you compare them with Burgundy, just up the road, they're positively cheap – and often a better drink. Rant over. This Brouilly has a delightful northern flavour of cold Scottish raspberries, a flicker of underripe peach, a strand or two of citrus peel, and an aftertaste like couturier's scented leather.

2005 Coteaux du Vendômois, Domaine de Montrieux, Loire Valley, France, 12.5% ABV
Les Caves de Pyrene, £10.20

I reckon these vines are the most northerly red variety to be grown in the Loire Valley. After this, just the long, aching schlep to Chartres Cathedral and the English Channel. So the air's cold, the soil – flints over limestone – is cold. And the flavour of the wine has a brilliant chill coursing through it. As soon as you smell

it – lead pencils, graphite, bay leaf and myrtle – you know the sun shines sparingly on these vines. Its flavour has a nice rasp of tannin, but much more grey, cold slate to temper the red cherry and red plum fruit – and the final impression is of lovely fresh summer earth in an English orchard after a light rain has knocked the apple blossom off the bough and onto the ground.

2006 The Fergus, Tim Adams, Clare Valley, South Australia, 14.5% ABV
Australian Wine Centre, Tesco, £10.20

The Fergus is a Tim Adams special based on century-old Grenache vines, but now adding Cabernet, Shiraz and Merlot to the blend. It isn't quite so wild and eucalyptus-laden as it used to be, but the eucalyptus is still there, along with a sprig or two of mint. The fruit is lush raspberry and loganberry that will sweeten with a little age, and it is nicely tempered with a mix of stones and dusty cream.

2006 Shiraz, Water Wheel Vineyards, Bendigo, Victoria, Australia, 16% ABV
Oz Wines, £9.99

Water Wheel is one of the great crowd-pleasers in the world of Aussie Shiraz. But the wines are not soft-centred juicy Lucys – this is a big brawny mouthful, but packed with peppermint and violet scent, sweet caramel oak smeared with tar and dense, purple sloes and ripe plum fruit. It packs some punch at 16%. It might have been even better at 14.5%.

2005 Syrah, Cerro Romauldo, Marmesa Vineyards, Edna Valley, California, USA, 14.5% ABV
Oddbins, £9.99

California planted a ridiculous amount of Syrah about a decade ago, thinking it was going to be the next big thing. But should they call it Syrah or Shiraz? Should it be bright and scented and French, or deep and pruney and South Australian? A lot of guys took the high-octane superripe route: impressive they may be, but I can't drink them. Edna Valley, though, is a small area, cool in California's terms, and Larry Brooks, Marmesa's winemaker, is a cool dude in anybody's terms. He likes to drink the stuff he makes, so this is quite deep, with some rich strawberry jam and red plum syrup and a little scented caramel – but it's not in overdrive; the second glass will beckon.

2004 Côtes du Ventoux, L'Archange, Domaine des Anges, Rhône Valley, France, 14.5% ABV
Big Red Wine, £9.95

I've known Domaine des Anges for ages, hidden up in the hills to the east of the Rhône Valley, and this is as good as anything they've produced. It has a ripe, rich smell of chocolate and plum, and a fascinating array of semi-conflicting flavours – blackberry and damson, milk chocolate, pepper and the rasp of herbs, even a hint of lime acidity – that truly evokes the warm wild hills of the Ventoux.

2006 Barbera d'Alba, Conca del Grillo, Silvano Bolmida, Piedmont, Italy, 14% ABV
Savage Selection, £9.80

Wow. This is impressive, almost brutish stuff. Italian reds need food: this positively demands it, screams for it, hopefully gets it, because it's definitely a wine you should serve *after* your guests have tucked into the main course, not before. It smells almost of the stableyard, though some weird perfume does peek through the steaming horsehide. And there is a dark, coiled core of bitter-sour-sweet fruit: rough black fruit and red sour cherry. Tunes? Phew! Pour me a Sauvignon, somebody.

2006 Chiroubles, Château de Javernand, Beaujolais, France, 12.5% ABV
Waterloo Wine, £9.60

I'm delighted to be including more Beaujolais in the guide this year; Javernand is an old favourite that has rediscovered its heart. Joyous, juicy, a delightful fruit salad of banana, strawberries and pale cherries, scattered with peppercorn and lightly bruised with stones.

2005 Minervois La Livinière, La Cantilène, Château Sainte-Eulalie, Languedoc, France, 14.5% ABV
The Wine Society, £9.50

Minervois is a large chunk of land, both flat and hilly, some good, some merely adequate, in France's far south. The choicest part is called La Livinière: the soils are all good here, and the land rises way into the hills above the plain. So La Livinière should be a guarantee of brighter, more perfumed wine. Château Sainte-Eulalie doesn't let you down. This has a marvellous hillside scent of basil and bay leaf and cracked black peppercorns. The herbs run right through the flavour too, tugging at the deep, ripe blackberry and black plum fruit and finishing off mingled with the dry scent of new leather.

2005 Rioja, Clisos, Federico Paternina, Spain, 13% ABV
Flagship Wines, £9.49

Paternina's Banda Azul used to be just about the biggest Rioja brand of all. I remember it from student days. It wasn't very good. Since then it's limped along in the shadows for ages, but in the last few years it's got a grip on itself and realized there's no place for a tired old slapper in the modern Rioja world. So this new Paternina manifestation is most welcome. The fruit is caught between red and black, but it's dense rather than delicate. And despite a splot of crème fraîche, the texture is mouthwateringly dry and grainy – pepper, savory and lovage battling it out with cedar and cigar tobacco for the upper hand.

2006 Côte de Brouilly, Domaine Georges Viornery, Beaujolais, France, 13% ABV
Haynes, Hanson & Clark, £9.45

Smashing stuff, and yet another reminder that Beaujolais is a brilliant drink and the good producers are making some of their best stuff for more than a decade. Beaujolais is a delight because it is rarely touched by new oak, and it doesn't attempt to be the biggest, most testosterone-thumping beast in the park. It's all about drinkability. This smells of red fruit and wood bark still on the tree. It has a lovely, soft, gentle raspberry flavour, soft Chelsea bun texture, with the ripple of a brook over pebbles keeping it dry and refreshing. At the end of a hard day's tasting, this was my choice.

2002 Rioja Reserva, Elegia, Taste the Difference (Torre de Oña), Spain, 13.5% ABV
Sainsbury's, £9.19

2002 isn't much of a vintage for Rioja, but Torre de Oña, owned by Rioja Alta, is a very good producer. Put the two together and you get lovely classy wine at a less than daunting price. This wine has a delightful mature style which would take years longer to develop from a stronger vintage. Easy-going, shiny leather and floral scent mixing with vanilla and coconut and gentle, restrained, strawberry fruit. Class.

2006 Old Vine Carignan, Vin de Pays de l'Aude, Cuvée Christophe, Domaine de la Souterranne, Languedoc, France, 14% ABV
The Oxford Wine Company, £8.99

I love seeing the word Carignan on a label. Carignan is one of the most traditional grapes in southern France, but over the generations has mostly been used as a high-yielding plonk blender. No one replants it, they'd rather rip it up and plant Merlot. But a few estates cherish it and have plantations stretching back a hundred years. When the vines are old, the yield drops dramatically and the flavour intensifies to a deep red – not black – minerally, herby syrup of flavour that seems to reflect the hillsides and rocks where the vines eke out their life. This is classic old Carignan: soft, deep red fruit, cranberry and redcurrant acidity, the rub of ancient stones and an enveloping film of glycerine and toffee.

2007 Côtes du Rhône, Château les Quatre Filles, Rhône Valley, France, 13.5% ABV Averys, £8.99

We should see more single-property Côtes du Rhônes. The trouble is, we associate the label 'Côtes du Rhône' with low-priced French basics, rather as we do the name 'Beaujolais', and consequently aren't willing to pay the higher price for single-vineyard wines. We should remember that these areas only became famous because there were really good single properties leading the way – and we should give them a chance to show how tasty their stuff is. These guys have been farming this vineyard since 1715. The wine has a heady sweet perfume of violets and loganberries, and although there's a bit of stony tannin, the feeling on your palate is of fresh, ripe raspberries and loganberries and the scent of summer.

2006 Decades (Shiraz-Cabernet-Merlot), Primo Estate, McLaren Vale, South Australia, 13.5% ABV Australian Wine Centre, £8.99

Powerful stuff. I'd expect nothing less from Joe Grilli at Primo Estate. Though his base is north of Adelaide, here he's using McLaren Vale fruit, from south of Adelaide. That fruit gives dense, strong wine, and Joe plays it well – rich mocha chocolate mousse texture trying to swamp the black, superripe, plummy fruit. But they shake hands and declare honours even in this muscular but soft-centred wine.

2005 Lirac, Domaine du Joncier, Rhône Valley, France, 14.5% ABV Waitrose, £8.99

This is made by a delightful titian-haired artist in the southern Rhône Valley. She used to concentrate on rosé, but my friend James May drank all her pink when we visited her to make a film. So now it's red. He can't drink that quite so fast. This is serious stuff. Lirac *is* quite serious – over the river from Châteauneuf-du-Pape – and this is deep and peppery and strewn with herbs, quite tannic too, but with a marvellous depth of blackberry and plum that will get sweeter if you leave it a year or two.

2006 Palo Alto Reserva, Maule Valley, Chile, 13.5% ABV
Threshers, Wine Rack, £8.99 (3 for 2, £5.99)

One smell of this and I thought, hey, this is going to be way too oaky. But never underestimate the power of Chilean fruit. You've got three very self-confident grape varieties here: Cabernet, Carmenère and Syrah. You can throw a lot of barrels at these three and they'll biff them to one side. Which is what happens here – the oaky mocha richness doesn't dominate the black plum, blackcurrant and celery freshness, and the chocolate richness is serious, all-enveloping, and very much at the core of the wine.

2006 Pinot Noir-Merlot, Ona, Anakena, Casablanca Valley, Chile, 14.5% ABV Oddbins, £8.99

I don't know anyone else who blends Merlot and Pinot Noir but, if I read the small print, that's not all. There's also 3% Syrah and 3% white Viognier. Well, I'm not complaining, because it works. I could see a hint of Viognier's golden cling peach, I could taste some Syrah smoke, but I think the Merlot does overpower the poor old Pinot. Or does it? I love the eucalyptus smell and the savoury, stewy, dark plum fruit, but the texture is very glyceriny – maybe *that's* the Pinot at work.

2007 Valpolicella, Allegrini, Veneto, Italy, 13% ABV
Bennetts, Hedley Wright, Liberty Wines, Stainton Wines, Valvona & Crolla, £8.99

Valpolicella is more like Italy's most infamous red, rather than its most famous. But if I had to award marks for sheer drinkability, Valpolicella would be at the top of Italy's tree. Real Valpolicella, that is, from the traditional hillside vineyards away from the agro-industry of the valley floor – and no one does it better than Allegrini. This is uplifting wine, perfectly balancing fresh and bitter and sour, white peach and red cherry jostling with juicy apple nipped with the bitterness of the pips and dusted off with soft summer earth.

Xavier, Vin de Table, France, 14% ABV
Big Red Wine Company, £8.95

Well, I've learned that this is a blend of eight grape varieties. But Xavier Vignon isn't allowed to give any information on the label, because this is a 'mere' vin de table. What the varieties are is still tasking me, but they're old French Rhône Valley performers on top form here. This has a fabulous aroma of Belgian milk chocolate that makes you think the wine will be soft and mellow, but it's strongly influenced by wind-blown stony dust and an insistent but surprisingly soft tannin. It has a fascinating wild hillside seasoning of bay, thyme and rosemary all badgering the dark mulberry, sloe and blackberry fruit. Visceral stuff, a mixture of mature and young, herb and fruit, tannin and softness, youthful vigour and the more contemplative snug bar mellowness of age.

2006 Tempranillo, Gazur, Telmo Rodríguez, Ribera del Duero, Spain, 13.5% ABV
Adnams, £8.50

Ribera del Duero near Valladolid grows some of my favourite red grapes in the whole of Spain, but usually they are soused in an excess of oak, and they're generally priced up to hell. But the supremely talented

Telmo Rodríguez doesn't get seduced by oak or silly money, he just revels in drawing out the best from his fruit. Here, he's created a dark, chewy wine, scented with plums ripe enough to drop, sweetened with black cherries, and with its glycerine heart packed round with stern tannin that will slowly melt away over the next couple of years.

2006 Cabernet Sauvignon, Cycles Gladiator, Central Coast, California, USA, 13.5% ABV
Flagship Wines, £8.49

There was a California brand called Rex Goliath on the shelves a few years ago which was lush, fruity and delightful. Shops sold out. The brand became a success. Too much of a success. A vast multinational bought it, changed the blend and the source of the grapes, threw tons of marketing money at it –

and, of course, that's the last I saw of it. But the grapes that used to go into the blend weren't wasted. They now make up Cycles Gladiator which, surprise, surprise, is just as good as Rex Goliath used to be, with rich black plum fleshiness, golden peach juiciness, the soothing texture of chocolate and a sprinkling of clove and cinnamon spice.

2006 Zinfandel, De Loach, California, USA, 14.5% ABV
Averys, Liberty Wines, Nickolls & Perks, Noel Young, £8.49

We should drink more good Zinfandel in this country – not white Zin, the pink sweet one, but hey, if you like it, drink it. But I'm talking real Zin, ripe, juicy, blue-collar America's red wine Zin. Well, we could start here. Zin should be come-hither, and this does the job: bright, misty, herby scent, rich fresh Victoria plum fruit mixed with good prune and syrup richness and a nice touch of acidity and mineral dust to show that this is a real red wine from a real place, not some pink junk from a factory half the size of New Zealand.

2006 Entraygues-le Fel, Olivier et Laurent Mousset, South-West France, 12.5% ABV
Caves de Pyrene, £8.05

If you're looking for the antidote to big, fat, alcoholic Australian Shiraz, look no further. This incredibly rare wine from South-West France – Entraygues is a tiny wine zone of only 22ha, mostly red, some white – shivers with the flavours of stones and cool sun and cold night air. Slate and graphite race across your palate, pursued by squashy raspberry fruit and apple and lemon zest acidity. If that sounds harsh, it isn't – it's bone dry but beautifully soft, fruity but sprinkled with mineral dust.

2006 Memsie (Shiraz-Cabernet Sauvignon-Malbec), Water Wheel, Bendigo, Victoria, Australia, 14.5% ABV   Oz Wines, £7.99

Water Wheel describe this as their lighter red blend. Lighter than what? Their rich, beefy Shiraz (see page 62), sure. But lighter than most other modern Aussie reds at £7.99? No way. This isn't a heavy wine, but it is lush and juicily fat. The smell of eucalyptus trees hangs in the glass. The flavour seems to have no hard edges: all blackberry and raspberry and toffee custard, the eucalyptus is still there, and some tannin does appear later on, but it doesn't get in the way of a final memory of home-baked coconut and treacle tart.

2006 Montepulciano d'Abruzzo, Torre Scalza, Abruzzo, Italy, 13.5% ABV
Marks & Spencer, £7.99

It isn't easy to find a good, plump, juicy Montepulciano. There should be loads of good grog – the Montepulciano is a wonderful juicy grape – but, sadly there isn't. M&S have been making a major effort in Italy recently, and they'll have sent their own winemakers down there to show the locals how to make the best out of their grapes. And here it is: low tannin, low acid (what? In Italy?), plump plum fruit, some creamy texture and just a hint of peach blossom.

2006 Petite Syrah, Teichert Ranch, Lodi, California, USA, 14% ABV
Marks & Spencer, £7.99

M&S have been making a considerable effort with their Californian wines, sourcing most of them from good, individual, family growers in less fashionable areas. It's paying off, with really tasty stuff at very fair prices. Lodi is an area inland towards Sacramento that is a particularly fertile hunting ground, and this wine is a four-square powerhouse. But it isn't simply muscle – there's violet and rosehip scent sitting daintily astride the dark, dense fruit and cream toffee oak. In fact, it has less gruff tannin than Petite Syrah almost always has. Well sniffed out, M&S.

2006 Ribera del Duero, El Quintanal, Quintana del Pidio, Castilla y León, Spain, 13% ABV
Oddbins, £7.99

A wine that shows it is possible to get lovely flavours at a fair price from what is probably Spain's finest – and most expensive – red wine region. This is attractively muscular, masculine wine, deep and dry, but with good ripe blackcurrant and black plum stuck in its heart. A touch of spice and a good burst of tannin makes this a top 'beefsteak medium rare' red.

2006 Shiraz, Barossa (St Hallett), South Australia, 14.5% ABV
Marks & Spencer, £7.99

This is the kind of Barossa Shiraz we used to see quite a bit of at this price level. It's a rare beast nowadays, but M&S have gone out and talked to the venerable St Hallett operation and put together a very good cuvée. It's loaded with coconut cream and vanilla, the fruit is a juicy dish of dark mulberry and loganberry, and the texture is gentle, deep and ripe. Why can't more £7.99 wines taste like this?

2006 Shiraz-Viognier, Zonte's Footstep, Langhorne Creek, South Australia, 14.5% ABV Somerfield, £7.99

Zonte's Footstep was created only a few years ago by some young guns intent upon maximizing the lush softness of Langhorne Creek fruit and charging a fair price. They upped the wine's juiciness by adding super-lush white Viognier to their plump Shiraz and have created a modern classic, offering utter pleasure, but also managing to be serious and deep. When you taste the wine, well, licorice is dark and serious, and maybe the herb scent is serious, but the rest – the blackberry, raspberry and loganberry fruit and the super gentle texture – that's just pure pleasure.

2005 Syrah, Cline Cellars, California, USA, 14% ABV Co-op, £7.99

A gentle giant. This smells of grilled meat and toasted nuts all jumbled up with rich black fruit. You start mentally lighting the barbecue. But it's actually softer than I expected. There is some ripe cranberry acidity, but mostly it's a tasty stew of chocolate and cocoa powder and squashy ripe black fruit. A good mouthful, if you like your reds a little floppy around the waistline.

2006 Dão, Quinta de Saes, Portugal, 13% ABV
Laymont & Shaw, £7.95

There was a time when Dão was Portugal's most famous red wine, but that was when there wasn't a lot of choice. Frankly, it was never much fun, fantastically dry and stony. But things have changed. Better grape varieties have been planted, the stranglehold of the co-operatives has been broken, and we're now at last seeing Dão's potential. This domaine is leading the charge. It's still a very dry wine, it's still stony and gaunt and reasonably tannic, but there is now a scent of damson and violet, the brooding purple fruit is now offset by cream and a sprinkling of clove and ginger. It's serious and impressive now. It'll be a lot better in a year or two.

2006 Shiraz, Heartland Wines, Langhorne Creek-Limestone Coast, South Australia, 14.5% ABV The Wine Society, £7.95

This label used to be dominated by grapes from a wild, off-the-beaten track vineyard at a one-horse-town called Wirrega. Now it's dominated by Langhorne Creek fruit and the style has lost its pungent eucalyptus character and gained a lush, loose-limbed personality more typical of Langhorne Creek. I do miss the eucalyptus, but this is lovely, deep, chocolaty red with syrupy black plums and teasing acidity making for a very attractive, easy-going Shiraz.

2006 Manjo Fango, Vin de Pays des Portes de Mediterranée, Les Terrasses d'Eole, Languedoc, France, 14% ABV
Lea and Sandeman, £7.75

Manjo Fango? The label helpfully explains that this means 'eat mud' in Provençal – but don't worry, it's not a tasting note. It's the name of a wind that 'eats mud' as it blows through the vineyards and dries them out. The wine is chewy and dense, but it's not muddy. What it does have is the new, as yet rare, but increasingly popular Marselan grape at its core, as well as Grenache to fatten it out and Mourvèdre to add a sense of southern wildness. This gives the wine a fruity thwack of dense plum syrup and prunes and some fairly chewy tannins, but it also keeps hold of a pear and apple freshness, and though the texture is dense, it's not impenetrable.

2007 Pinot Noir, Reserva, Cono Sur, Casablanca Valley, Chile, 14% ABV
Somerfield, Tesco, £7.69

Cono Sur Pinot Noir was a great stalwart at £4.99 for some years – never thrilling, but always soft and gentle and *very* Pinot. Well, this is the Reserve bottling, using better grapes from better vineyards, and it's a big leap in quality. It has a lovely lush but fresh texture, soft red plum and cherry fruit balanced by pleasantly tart acidity. It manages to be fresh and juicy and mellow all at once.

2004 Saint Chinian, Château Bousquette, Languedoc, France, 13.5% ABV Connolly's, £7.40

Saint Chinian is divided into two zones: one makes attractive, quite soft reds; the other is altogether more burly and boisterous. This is the boisterous sort – you can feel the rocks in the wine, you can smell the bay leaf and sage, the fennel and the leather. But the flavour is rich and red, raspberries and plums, blackened up a little by bittersweet licorice.

2007 Teroldego delle Venezie, Novello delle Vivene, Trentino, Italy, 12% ABV Laithwaites, £7.39

We're so keen on bright, tangy, fresh white wines, I'd have thought we should be prepared to give mouthwatering, frisky reds a go too. But we don't accord them the same enthusiasm at all. Which is a pity, because cherry-red gluggers like this can be chilled down and are just as refreshing as whites. You get a kind of summer pudding of flavours – mulberries, blackberries, strawberry, banana and pear – but you also get a good stony dry rasp and redcurrant acidity to keep it tangy and revivifying.

2006 South African Pinotage, The Best, 13% ABV Morrisons, £7.20

Pinotage has flavours like no other red wine. It also has the ability to make perfectly rational red wine lovers go apoplectic at the mere mention of the name. Surely not if it tastes as nice as this – bright mulberry fruit with some mild chocolaty smoke and a softness of toasted marshmallows, with a little raisin toffee to finish off, and *not* too much tannin. What's to loathe about that?

2006 Bonarda Reserve, Santa Rosa, Familia Zuccardi, Mendoza, Argentina, 13% ABV
Oddbins, £6.99

Bonarda could easily be Argentina's Beaujolais, and Bonarda Reserve could easily do the job of Beaujolais' top 'Cru' villages. There's a lot of Bonarda in the vineyards, and it makes such a juicy, gluggable red. This one mixes wild strawberry scent with redcurrant and red plum fruit and a trail of mineral dust; it is one of Argentina's most refreshing reds.

2003 Cabernet Sauvignon Reserva, El Huique, Colchagua Valley, Chile, 14% ABV The Chilean Wine Club, £6.99

Juicy, grainy, slightly loose-knit but consequently very easy to enjoy. This is what Chile's warm, fertile Colchagua region should do more of. Rich damsons and blackberry are not typically Cabernet flavours, but they're very attractive, and when some earthy dryness pops up, along with blackcurrant – *that's* classic Cabernet – and Cox's apple acid – that's *not* – with a hint of crème fraîche softness to round it out – well, if it isn't *that* typical, so what?

2006 Carmenère (organic), Adobe, Viñedos Emiliana, Colchagua Valley, Chile, 14.5% ABV Majestic Wine, £6.99

On first smell I wasn't so sure: this comes from an organic vineyard – had they taken 'The Good Life' practices too far? Just taste it. Any hint at over-natural methods is blown away by a typhoon of deep black fruit and the Carmenère's calling card: coal smoke, stewed celery and coffee beans, soy sauce and peppercorn. Rich black fruit, deep savoury scents. And the fruit's organic.

2006 Carmenère, Punto Niño, Laroche, Colchagua Valley, Chile, 14.5% ABV Booths, £6.99

When a French company like Laroche arrives in Chile, I worry that they may try to tame the native flavours and ape French styles. Luckily, Laroche make this wine as though they're thrilled by the sheer difference the Carmenère offers, and they let it rip – celery and peppercorn and soy sauce piled in with rich black fruit, herb scent, grainy tannin and, wrapping it all up, a surprisingly waxy, round texture.

2007 Corbières (organic), Château Pech-Latt, Languedoc, France, 14% ABV Waitrose, £6.99

This is still very young, and I wondered at first if it was a bit too fierce. Then I thought, no, it *is* impressive and powerful, but it isn't too dense to enjoy now, and it will mellow and soften to a beautiful waxy-textured red fruit syrup of fine old Carignan vines in a year or two. So you can leave it to ripen like a good cheddar cheese, or you can enjoy it now, for its rich, broad-shouldered plum fruit and its texture and aroma of the rough, lonely Corbières hills.

2006 Merlot, Vin de Pays de l'Aude, Cuvée Guillaume, Domaine de la Souterranne, Languedoc, France, 14% ABV
The Oxford Wine Company, £6.99

Take a beautiful old wine estate in an unfashionable area, give it new English owners and co-opt Aussie David Morrison as a consultant, and … bingo – great flavours, great style, sensible prices. So many French Merlots are dull. Not this one. It's throwing off clouds of blackberry, blackcurrant and mint aroma, and has blended a serious, chewy texture with utterly delightful ripe black fruit and mint and herb seasoning. Just what Merlot ought to be.

2007 Pinot Noir, Winemaker Reserva, Porta, Viñedos y Bodegas Córpora, Bío Bío Valley, Chile, 14% ABV
Wine Rack, £6.99 (3 for 2, £4.66)

This is good value at full price, but if you keep in mind the three for the price of two offer, the cost comes right down to a best in the High Street £4.66. For that you get a very serious Pinot, with a sloe-eyed eucalyptus and black cherry perfume and a deep flavour that does have a tannic edge, but easily makes up for it with resiny scent and black, sweet fruit.

2006 Pontificis, Grenache-Syrah-Mourvedre, Vin de Pays d'Oc, Laurent Delaunay, Languedoc, France, 13.5% ABV Averys, £6.99

A wine named after the pontiff? Well, to be honest, it does taste mightily like the Châteauneuf-du-Pape of the fresher, fruitier variety, and it is a blend of the right grapes. It's not from the right area, however, and it's *far* too cheap. Good. So let's lap up the sweet blackcurrant and blackberry fruit that reels backwards and forwards towards strawberry and raspberry and is tied together with nice taut acidity.

2006 Tinta da Ânfora, VR Alentejano, Bacalhôa Vinhos de Portugal, 14% ABV
Majestic Wine, Sainsbury's, Waitrose, £6.99

It's a slow business trying to persuade the British that their oldest and most constant friends in Europe, the Portuguese, are now making some of the most drinker-friendly wines on the Continent. And the most interesting. And the most affordable. They've got a whole pile of grape varieties that taste great but that no one's ever heard of, and they have a healthy disdain towards attempts to 'internationalize' the flavours of their wines. This is a dense, stewy, ultra-fruity wodge of a wine – blackberries and the burnt bit at the edge of strawberry jam tarts, crumble pastry and a dark Stygian syrup. Ânfora used to be well-known here. Welcome back, old friend.

2006 Cabernet Sauvignon, Casillero del Diablo, Concha y Toro, Central Valley, Chile, 13.5% ABV
widely available, £6.99

This is a triumph. Not just because the wine is good, but also because you can get it in every High Street in the land, at wine stores, off-licences and supermarkets. Concha y Toro are Chile's biggest producer. Casillero del Diablo is their fighting brand; it just shows big brands don't have to be bland rubbish. This is powerful, serious, dark black fruit with a spine of ripe tannin and a light brush of herbs. Excellent.

2005 Faugères, Le 1er, Château Haut Lignières, Languedoc, France, 13% ABV
Majestic Wine, £6.49

Faugères makes famously juicy reds in the south of France. I remember my first tasting of a bunch of wines from the village, smuggled in among a throng of thin, dry, raw neighbours, and being thrilled by the dark juicy fruit of the Faugères. This doesn't disappoint in the fruit department – there's loads of soft blackberry and black cherry to enjoy – but it is drier than many examples, attractively so, and scented with a good swirl of bay leaf perfume.

2007 Carmenère, Gamma, Viñedos Emiliana, Colchagua Valley, Chile, 14.5% ABV
Oddbins, £6.49

Sensational stuff, worth twice the money. Not only is it made by one of Chile's greatest winemakers, but the fruit is all organic, from a vineyard I visited last year that is like a paradise, it's so full of wildlife and nature's variety. I wanted to spend the whole day there, drifting in the calm tranquillity that seemed to pervade the vineyard. Tasting the wines was a revelation too, because Emiliana makes several tiers of quality above this one, yet for sheer impressive drinkability this can't be beat. The Carmenère is a brilliant grape, Chile's calling card, bursting with personality. Wonderfully rich and dense, dark ripe blackcurrant fruit swirled about with pepper, celery, chocolate and soy sauce and dusted with cocoa. Beat that.

AROUND £5

It will be interesting to see what happens to the prices of wines at about a fiver. Retailers know the power of pricing a wine at just a penny below a five pound note. It's such a simple proposition. Hand over a fiver and we'll give you a bottle that you can be assured will be pretty decent stuff. And a penny change. The trouble is that the £4.99 slot then gets bunged up with stuff from the big companies who have spent their money on labels, advertising, promotions, etc., and not on the quality in the bottle. So £4.99 becomes a cliché price point. Last year I was pretty lax with the definition of a fiver and there were some wines at £5.50 or more, simply because they were excellent and real value for money. Well, quite a few of last year's £5.50 wines have gone to nearer six quid this year and, rather than leave them out, I've spread the net a bit more. After all, which would you rather I did? Stick rigidly to the fiver rule, or include thrilling stuff for just under six quid?

- In this section you will find white wines first, then reds, in descending price order.

WHITE WINE

2006 Riesling, Steillage, Tesco Finest, Mosel, Germany, 11% ABV
Tesco, £6.19

The Steillagen are the terrifyingly steep vineyards that tumble down to the Mosel river in Germany. All the best wines come from these vertiginous vines. There's already an exodus of young people from the valley, unwilling to work in the vineyards under such tough conditions, however good the resultant wine. Enthusiastic Poles fill their place now, but as Poland becomes more prosperous there is a real chance no one will be bothered to slave away on these slatey slopes. So enjoy it while you can. This gentle, soft, light wine, fluffy apple flesh and white peach swapping flavours with creamy leather softness, and a tinkling acidity dancing between lemon zest, slate and freshly cut herbs, shows why you should care about these vineyards.

2007 Riesling, Tingleup, Tesco Finest, Howard Park, Great Southern, Western Australia, 13% ABV Tesco, £6.19

Good value, this. Really nice sharp lime scent and good lime zest and green apple flavour. The grapes were grown in the far south of Western Australia and wines from this outpost of Aussie brilliance do have a very gentle texture. Ally that softness to the sharp green flavours and you've got a delicious glass of Riesling.

2004 Riesling Kabinett, Trierer Deutschherrenberg, Deutschherrenhof, Mosel, Germany, 8% ABV
Majestic Wine, £5.99

I love the name Deutschherrenberg. 'The German gentleman's mountain'. Very precise and correct. And the producer's name is 'Oberbillig'. Forgive my German, but doesn't that mean 'too cheap'? Well then, dash down to Majestic before they put the price up. And if you've given up on German wines as dull sugar-water, this is the reason to give them another chance. I know the name's a mouthful, but you don't have to pronounce it. Just take this book into Majestic and point. Even if the staff gave you the wrong bottle it wouldn't matter that much because Majestic have the best range of high-quality low-priced German wines of anyone in the country. And they do this light, fragile but succulent Mosel style particularly well. It has a heather honey semi-sweetness, a soothing texture of brioche or cream bun softness and a delightful streak of lemon-zest mineral acidity. And it's only 8% alcohol.

2007 Vinho Verde, Quinta de Azevedo, Portugal, 11% ABV
Majestic Wine, Waitrose, £5.99

Vinho Verde has never had much of a reputation in the UK – mostly because the commercial brands were over-sulphured sugared-up rubbish. But the real, single-estate Vinho Verde is an absolute delight – startlingly dry, yet quite different from wines like Chablis or Sauvignon, and sometimes with a refreshing prickle to back up the lean acidity. This one does prickle on the tongue, and manages to be sharp yet not raw, with a marvellous revivifying marriage of melon, banana and pear fruit streaked with the juice and the pith of ripe grapefruit. Loads of flavour and a tongue-cleansing rasp. All that, and only 11% alcohol.

2006 Colombard-Ugni Blanc, Vin de Pays des Côtes de Gascogne, Beaulieu, South-West France, 11.5% ABV Savage Selection, £5.95

The classic Gascony grape variety mix: two sharp grapes, both eager to ensnare the other in its tangy embrace. This example is relatively soft and has a touch of anis scent, but the core of the pleasure is grapefruit acidity, apple flesh and the rasp of lemon pith – in mellower mood than is often the case.

2007 Vin de Pays des Côtes de Gascogne, La Courtine, Producteurs Plaimont, South-West France, 11.5% ABV Christopher Piper, £5.70

The Armagnac region of South-West France has been making sharp, tangy, fruity and affordable dry white wines for a generation, and Plaimont have been the leading producers all this time. They make lots of different cuvées and Christopher Piper has picked a good one, full of the flesh of green fruit – apple and kiwi and greengage – as well as lemon zest brightness and a hint of applemint perfume.

2006 The Society's Chardonnay, Concha y Toro, Casablanca Valley, Chile, 13.5% ABV The Wine Society, £5.50

There are some things that never change in the wine world, and one of them is the quality and style of the Wine Society's Chilean Chardonnay. It's as old-fashioned and as unruffled by the foibles of fashion as ever. But I like that. Too many modern Chardonnays seem to have lost confidence in themselves, while this one exudes pineapple syrup softness, apple purée richness and acid, and toasted nuts oak. Real, unmistakable Chilean Chardie.

2007 Sauvignon-Verdejo, Casa del Sol, Agricola Castellana, Castilla y León, Spain, 13% ABV Co-op, £5.49

Verdejo is often touted as Spain's answer to the Sauvignon grape, but it actually tastes much better when it asks Sauvignon for a bit of help. Verdejo fundamentally has a green, grapefruity flavour and a soft texture. It usually needs some extra zip, and here the Sauvignon adds nettle, green apple and lime sharpness without overpowering the Verdejo's gentle nature.

2007 Muscadet Sèvre et Maine sur lie, Taste the Difference (Domaine Jean Douillard), Loire Valley, France, 12% ABV Sainsbury's, £4.99

Sainsbury's Taste the Difference Muscadet has been one of their most reliable performers over the years, and the 2007 vintage is no exception. Except that it doesn't taste like typical Muscadet – it has more personality! This one is *very* fruity, piled with crisp apple, peach and pear juice flavours and attractively sharp acidity. Enough to give Muscadet a good name again.

2007 Sauvignon Blanc, Stellar Organics, Fairtrade, Western Cape, South Africa, 12.5% ABV Asda, Booths, £4.99

I've liked the Stellar people since the first time I met them, and they're on a learning curve that's heading rapidly *up*. This is very nice, classy, affordable Sauvignon from South Africa's West Coast. It's a fabulous area for Sauvignon: we'll be seeing a lot more pretty soon. It's got a bright, sharp taste – coffee beans and nettles, green pepper and apple peel – that can start to give New Zealand a real run for its money.

2006 Chenin-Chardonnay, Vin de Pays des Côtes de Gascogne, Domaine du Tariquet, South-West France, 12% ABV Booths, £4.89

Chenin and, especially, Chardonnay, are world-famous varieties which grow well in Gascony – it's just that no one had thought to try. But anything with Chardonnay in the title is easy to sell, which explains this blend. And it works nicely, with the sharp tang of Gascony more evident than the flavour of any particular grape variety. Grapefruity acidity, apple flesh flecked with minerals and mellow lemon scent make for a good drink.

2007 Pinot Grigio, Hilltop Neszmély, Neszmély, Hungary, 12.5% ABV Marks & Spencer, £4.79

Pinot Grigio is not usually a wine that has much flavour – sadly, that's probably one of the reasons it's so successful. But the grape variety is a very good one and when sold as Pinot *Gris* often has loads of character. Neszmély's example is still Grigio in style in that it's soft and mild – but within that softness is a delightful flavour and texture of soft fluffy apple flesh, some gentle green apple peel acidity, and a hint of orchard blossom and anis scent.

2006 Vin de Pays des Côtes de Gascogne, Harmonie de Gascogne, Domaine de Pellehaut, South-West France, 12% ABV Booths, £4.49

Pellehaut are one of my favourite producers in Gascony. They are true innovators in the region, not content simply to use the old traditional grape varieties, so here we get a mix of Colombard and Ugni (traditional) with Gros Manseng, Chardonnay and Sauvignon (not traditional but well suited to the area). And they've also put some oak barrels to use, which reduces the freshness but increases the depth and complexity, so that the wine ends up tasting like something much more expensive from the smart Pessac-Léognan area of Bordeaux. It mixes leafy sharpness with old autumn fruit – peaches and medlars with dried-out withered skins – and a soft creaminess like baked rice pudding.

RED WINE

2006 Salice Salentino, Feudi di San Marzano, Puglia, Italy, 13% ABV
Tanners, £6.30

Things are looking up in the heel of Italy. They've been making good, mature, attractively predictable reds down there for some years, but Salice Salentino clearly isn't satisfied with simply churning out the same old recipe and is reaching for the challenge of making a more youthful red style. They've got excellent grape varieties down there, but it's only now we're seeing them in their bright, brash, youthful glory. This one's a big beast, the fruit almost baked black, the herbs bleached by the harsh southern sun. But it's good, and it'll age too.

2006 Cabernet Sauvignon, Luis Felipe Edwards, Colchagua Valley, Chile, 14% ABV Tesco, £6.19

Luis Felipe Edwards is a large winery undergoing a transformation, and this is its new face. It has access to lots of soft, ripe Colchagua fruit – the problem in the past has been maintaining the grapes' freshness and keeping that bright, fresh fruit in the wines. Well, this looks good. It has dense blackcurrant and black plum fruit, with drifting coal smoke and ripe, strong tannin. If you want your Cabernet big and thrusting but full of fruit – and cheap – this is for you.

2005 Rioja Tinto Crianza, Viña Caña, Spain, 13% ABV
Somerfield, £6.09

Somerfield seems to have a secret code when it comes to sourcing real Rioja at a fair price. This has gentle strawberry fruit, slightly bruised maybe, peach flesh just drying out a little, the peach stone adding a little hardness without being rough, and a brioche bready cream, saying, here it is, adults' red wine without tears.

2007 Cabernet Sauvignon-Carmenère, Porta Reserva, Viñedos y Bodegas Córpora, Chile, 14% ABV
Threshers, Wine Rack, £5.99 (3 for 2, £3.99)

When Chilean wines are this good this cheap you begin to wonder just how good they can be for a few quid more. Well, better, for sure, but better value? No, you simply can't beat Chile for real value at this price. The Carmenère actually manages to dominate the Cabernet – which is rare, because Cabernet is a bully of a grape – and it does so with a torrent of black plum, chocolate, sweet celery and a whiff of violets all wrapped in oak spice.

2006 Côtes du Rhône Villages, Taste the Difference (M Chapoutier), Rhône Valley, France, 14% ABV
Sainsbury's, £5.99

Chapoutier is on fire at the moment. It's a big outfit – it owns more vineyard land in the Rhône Valley than anyone else – and it *could* get away with good but uninspiring blends for a label like Côtes du Rhône Villages. But I've had several examples recently, particularly from the 2006 and 2007 vintages, of exceptional wine under a potentially humdrum appellation. This is exactly what you'd want from a Rhône red: loads of ripe, rich black cherry and red plum fruit, noticeable bay-leaf scent and a grainy tannin to give a fruity but chewy character to the wine.

nv Il Fagiano, Vino da Tavola Rosso, Italy, 13% ABV
Averys, £5.99

Italian reds are famous for demanding food. Sometimes this simply means that they're pretty undrinkable by themselves, and as such don't get into a guide like this one. But other wines are full of flavour yet just cry out for a plateful of edibles to make them taste even better. That's the case here. It's a powerful wine, deep, dense cherry sauce and chewy toffee roughed up with tannin and splashed with coffee and herbs. Now bring on the *bistecca*.

2007 Vin de Pays du Gard (organic), Saint Roche, Domaine de Tavernel, Languedoc, France, 13.5% ABV
Waitrose, £5.99

Dark, deep, perfumed wine, just what the south of France can do so well, but does too infrequently. This is rich without being overripe, juicy but also chewy, with a flavour of black cherry flesh and a scent like the bloom on grape skins at harvest time. Yum.

2005 Salice Salentino, La Masseria, Cantine di San Marzano, Puglia, Italy, 13% ABV
Wine Rack, £5.99 (3 for 2, £3.99)

I've always expected Salice Salentino, from the heel of Italy, to be a soothing, rich, brownish kind of red, traditional to its boots, mellow and sunburnt, yearning towards the past, not bouncing towards the future. And then I find this – a bright, fresh, totally modern version of the old favourite. I'm amazed. It's a lovely, gluggable, juicy red from the last place I would expect to produce it; ripe, youthful banana scent bounces about with strawberry and red cherry syrup and a nip of tannin. In the far distance I can sense a touch of traditional tobacco scent and prune-skin richness, but it's a long way away.

2007 Shiraz, Jindalee Circle Collection, Jindalee Estate/Littore Family Estate, South Eastern Australia, 14% ABV
Morrisons, Waitrose, £5.99

Jindalee is one of those secondary brands that you don't see piled high on gondola ends braying for your attention, and usually offering you half-price deals. Thank goodness for small mercies, because few of those big discount brands bother to keep quality up, whereas Jindalee has kept things going pretty well over the years. This has juicy black plum fruit and that strange but delicious sensation you get when you add cream to stewed plums and it curdles. Add a little spice and decent acidity and you've got a rare, enjoyable, example of an endangered species – Australian budget Shiraz.

2006 Tempranillo-Cabernet Sauvignon, Sequiot, Valencia, Spain, 14.5% ABV
The Halifax Wine Company, Liberty Wines, Nickolls & Perks, £5.95

I know Valencia for its oranges and its cheap, gooey but tasty Moscatel wines, *not* for its appetizing reds. Well, maybe I'll need to reset my radar, because this is good stuff – dark plum fruit stirred up with honey and raisin richness and scented with thyme and rosemary – that manages to stay fresh and juicy despite high alcohol and an unmistakable warm-climate style.

2007 Rioja, Zuazo Gaston, Spain, 13% ABV
Waterloo Wine, £5.75

I'm beginning to see quite a few really tasty Riojas creeping onto our shelves from producers I really don't know, but at prices I like. Now this is *very* young for a Rioja, but the Tempranillo grape that makes up most of the Rioja blend has always been brilliant as a youthful glugger, as well as being ideally suited to aging. I'm sure this would age – but why? With a deep purple juiciness that also has some chewy grip, with a creamy texture, lush red and black plum fruit and yet some quite toothy tannin and a flicker of tobacco and apple peel – well, it's too good to age.

nv Claret – The Best, Maison Sichel, Bordeaux, France, 12.5% ABV
Morrisons, £5.25

I didn't expect to find many drinkable Bordeaux reds at this price level, but Morrisons have gone to Sichel, a respected Bordeaux producer, and come up with this tasty red: slightly rough fruit and typical Bordeaux earthy stones, but the real thing.

2006 Beaujolais, Cuvée des Vignerons, Cave des Vignerons de Bully, Burgundy, France, 12.5% ABV
Waitrose, £4.99

Beaujolais is a simple wine. Any attempt to add unnecessary complexity usually results in the wine's simple brilliance being muddied, its essential joyous, innocent exuberance being corrupted by a seriousness it doesn't request or deserve. Luckily the producers have not complicated this: easy, gentle, raspberry fruit, a soft, fresh pear flesh scent and a rattle of pebbles to cleanse your tongue.

2007 Carmenère, Los Robles, Fairtrade, Curico Valley, Chile, 13.5% ABV
Asda, £4.99; Sainsbury's, Waitrose, £5.49

The wine that made us take Fairtrade wine seriously. Each year I worry that they'll change it, that some consultant will come in and say, hey, people don't like that peppercorn, soy sauce, savoury style, let's make it fatter and softer – and duller. But they just keep barrelling on. Don't change, fellas. Keep making this tasty delight, full of dark blackcurrant fruit, peppercorns and celery and coffee beans – and keep using the Fairtrade premium to lift more people outof poverty.

2006 Garnacha, Vineyard X, Bodegas Borsao, Aragón, Spain, 13.5% ABV
Threshers, Wine Rack, £4.99 (3 for 2, £3.33)

Buy three of these, pay for two, and you've got one of the best red wine buys on the High Street. Rich juicy strawberries and slightly bruised cooked cherries, a handful of stones and a sprig of thyme and rosemary. Great party red, but good enough for the Sunday lunch table.

2006 Vin de Pays de Vaucluse, Les Rives d'Alcion, Domaine André Brunel, Languedoc, France, 14% ABV
Majestic Wine, £4.99

A wine that comes with a health warning. Do not approach if you are of a delicate disposition. This is no shrinking violet. The flavour is excellent – deep lush blackberry fruit and breezy bay leaf and basil scent – as you'd expect from M. Brunel, who is a leading producer of Châteauneuf-du-Pape. But it is brutally tannic, so don't drink it by itself. However, you *can* tame the tannin in red wines. Drink them with underdone beef or lamb, or drink them with hard British or Dutch cheeses – both will dissolve the tannins in your mouth. The meat will enhance the wine's character, the cheese will try to dominate it. But I'd bet on this beautiful beast coming through unscathed.

2005 Syrah, Vin de Pays de l'Ardèche, Cave Saint-Désirat, Rhône Valley, France, 12% ABV
Booths, £4.49

Syrah makes the great and famous northern Rhône reds such as Côte-Rôtie and Hermitage, expensive and delicious. But only a mile or two to the west, the Syrah still grows well, yet it can't be called anything but Vin de Pays. Which is our good fortune: this example has classic cool Syrah flavours – smoky blackberry, some sweet root vegetable like well-cooked swede, and attractive, appetizing acid and tannin. Classy, lean, affordable.

CHEAP AND CHEERFUL

I wonder if the Government has finally done it. Killed off the £2.99 bottle. Frankly, the 14p per bottle duty rise in the 2008 budget should have knocked £2.99 wine on the head, because when you add VAT and 'administrative charges' – honest, the supermarkets add an admin fee for changing the price! – most £2.99ers should be £3.19, and once you're at £3.19, why not go to £3.49 and gobble up a bit of profit along the way? But I swear the £2.99 wine will still be here at Christmas, because some of the big producers are so desperate for business they swallow the 14p duty rise. But they don't make 14p profit on a bottle of £2.99 wine! The power of the supermarkets to shift booze continues unabated. Anyway, this section is more about £3.99, and a bit over, because I'm much keener to get you to spend an extra quid on a better bottle of wine than wear out my liver and my brain scraping the bottom of the wine barrel. Even so, there is the odd wine around three quid which is pretty decent. Enjoy it while you prepare to trade up.

- In this section you will find white wines first, then reds, in descending price order.

WHITE WINE

2007 Torrontes-Chardonnay, Tierra Brisa, Filus, Mendoza, Argentina, 13% ABV
Majestic Wine, £4.79

Torrontes is a wildly floral Argentine grape, whereas Chardonnay can be a bit neutral in the torrid fields beneath the Andes. A sensible marriage then, and the result is a gentle, balanced white, soft yet zesty, mildly floral but kept in check by ripe grapefruit and a little lemon rind.

2007 Verdicchio dei Castelli di Jesi Classico, Moncaro, Marche, Italy, 12.5% ABV
Waitrose, £4.69

Nice, full, fat, soft Italian white, with a bit of syrupy richness and fruit like a baked apple tart. But it isn't sweet, it's pretty dry, just squidgy at the hips.

2007 Chenin-Chardonnay, Fuzion, Familia Zuccardi, Mendoza, Argentina, 13% ABV
Somerfield, £4.19

It isn't easy to make fresh, bright, modern whites under Mendoza's baking skies, but José Zuccardi is the past master of value-for-money wines there, and if he can't do it, nobody can. This isn't completely dry, but the flavour is a delightful pale fruit salad of white melon, mild peach and a slice or two of banana.

2007 Chardonnay, Coldridge Estate, McGuigan Simeon Wines, South Eastern Australia, 12.5% ABV
Majestic Wine, £3.99

Pretty good commercial Aussie Chardie. Doesn't seem completely dry – and it probably isn't – but it has nice ripe apple fruit and some pretty juicy Florida grapefruit acidity topped off with a little oak spice and creamy texture.

2006 Colombard-Chardonnay, Jindu, South Eastern Australia, 12.5% ABV
Waitrose, £3.99

I don't come across many attractive cheap Aussie whites any more – most of them have been sweetened up and dumbed down beyond recognition. But this one's good: mild banana and fluffy apple fruit with a touch of golden cling peach and some green apple acidity giving it a bit of tingle.

2007 Vieille Fontaine, Vin de Pays du Gers, Plaimont/Producteurs Vignoble de Gascogne, South-West France, 11.5% ABV
Tesco, £3.40

Each year I check out Tesco's French cheapo, and each year it delivers. It's made by an excellent co-op in Gascony and is a bright, leafy, green apple and pear wine, with a little earthiness to stop it having any fancy ideas.
+ The Vieille Fontaine red is good too.

2007 Chardonnay, Valle Central, Chile, 13% ABV
Asda, £3.18

Asda have made quite a speciality of their basic Chileans, and now they've given them cool 'transport motif' labels – this one's got a metro train on it – they look pretty good on your table as well. It's a simple, fresh, scented style with pear and apple and some lemon acid. Very nice.

+ The Merlot and Cabernet Sauvignon are pretty decent too.

RED WINE

2006 Bonarda, Dios del Sol, Mendoza, Argentina, 12.5% ABV
Somerfield, £4.19

Somerfield have clearly done their homework on Argentina. Bonarda is very widely planted, but almost unknown in the UK; wines like this should help. It's got squashy wild strawberry and apple fruit, just dried out a little by high summer dust and a nip of tannin.

2007 Shiraz-Malbec, Fuzion, Familia Zuccardi, Mendoza, Argentina, 13% ABV
Somerfield, £4.19

Made by the excellent Zuccardi winery, this is the kind of Argentine basic we should see much more of, because Argentine conditions are perfect for good, fairly priced reds. This has a beguiling gentle style, plum and blackberry fruit, lightened up and perfumed with pears.

2006 Campo de Borja Tinto, Gran López, Crianzas y Viñedos Santo Cristo, Aragón, Spain, 13% ABV
Waitrose, £3.99

Campo de Borja is possibly Spain's best source of chunky, richly fruity reds. This one's chunky all right, with deep, raspberry sauce richness and a swish of herbs to freshen it up and stop it becoming gloopy.

2006 Carignan Old Vines, Vin de Pays de l'Aude, Le Sanglier de la Montagne, Les Caves du Mont Tauch, Languedoc, France, 12.5% ABV
Booths, £3.99

This wine is called 'The wild boar of the mountain'. But don't think the wine is a beast – it isn't. It's barely more than a gruff pussycat. Carignan *can* be a rough grape, but these guys have moulded a delightful, gently jammy wine tasting of stewed rosehip, sweet sloes and red plum, seasoned with bay and thyme, and sharpened by the mellow acid of boiled lemons.

2006 Corbières, Réserve de la Perrière, Les Caves du Mont Tauch, Languedoc, France, 13% ABV
Waitrose, £3.99

The hills of Corbières are magnificent and wild, savage at times, and the wines can be the same – impressive, but your tongue may need to be wearing a flak jacket. But this version is positively gentle. It's got lots of squashy, almost stewy, red fruit but manages to remain juicy and fresh and not remotely terrifying.

2005 Shiraz-Cabernet, Jindu, South Eastern Australia, 13% ABV
Waitrose, £3.99

Good flavours here, although they would have been better if they were a bit more intense. Still, we are talking £3.99, so a bit of dilution of the attractive chocolate and plum richness is perhaps only to be expected.

2006 Beaujolais, France, 12% ABV
Asda, £3.76

I take my hat off to Asda for this one. Beaujolais should be a bright, refreshing, affordable, everyday red, but it has priced itself out of the market, with the result that most people have stopped buying it. Well, perhaps this will persuade them to start again. It comes from a good co-operative in a decent village, Quincié, and is bright, simple, refreshing – stones and strawberries and pearskins – and low in alcohol. Drink it cool and often.

2007 South African Cabernet-Shiraz (Swartland Winery), 13.5% ABV
Tesco, £3.69

A 50:50 blend of Cabernet Sauvignon and Shiraz. It's a blend perfected by the Aussies in the good old days, but the South Africans obviously understand it: this has good, rich, juicy fruit, a bit of stony dryness and an enticing veil of Shiraz smoke.

2006 Vin de Pays de l'Hérault, Cuvée Chasseur, Les Producteurs Réunis, Languedoc, France, 12% ABV
Waitrose, £3.29

An old favourite that never lets me down. Full, soft, gentle, bright red, flowing with red plum and apple fleshiness, dead easy to drink and very light on the pocket. If I had a quibble, I'd wonder if it has become slightly less dry over the years.
+ The white version, Cuvée Pêcheur, is also good.

2007 Garnacha, Gran Tesoro, Bodegas Borsao, Campo de Borja, Aragón, Spain, 13.5% ABV
Tesco, £3.19

Wow, these guys at Bodegas Borsao are good. They're located bang in the middle of nowhere except vast fields of superripe old Garnacha grapes. And they know how to make the best of them. Here's a fabulous juicy mix of raspberry fruit and syrup, slightly enriched with warm raisins, and toughened up with rosemary, pepper and thyme. Brilliant, chewy, super-fruity glugger.
+ Other retailers also use Borsao for their budget Spanish red, so look for the name in the small print.

ROSÉ WINES

People want pink. They want it cold. They want it in copious quantities. And they want it sweet. What? Surely not? Well, the surge in drinking pink that has seen sales rise by up to 100% in some retailers and bars has been led by White Zinfandel from California. That's the sweet, bland, pink mouthwash in which the taste of sugar outweighs the taste of the grape. But although the growth is led by them, the other categories of really good, tasty and generally dry pinks are also proving hugely popular. So here's my choice.

• The wines are listed in descending price order.

2006 Côtes de Provence, Les Fenouils, Domaine de Jale, Provence, France, 12.5% ABV
Goedhuis & Company, £9.30

Spot-on Provence rosé. It's lighter, more fluffy than the Domaine Sainte Lucie (below), but just right if you like your pink bone dry, flecked with the acidity of lemons and rubbed with the austere freshness of pebbles.

2007 Sangiovese Rosé, Eldredge Vineyards, Clare Valley, South Australia, 13.5% ABV
Australian Wine Centre, £8.99

You often have to go outside Italy to see red Italian grape varieties in a come-hither mood. This is the Chianti Classico grape, from the Clare Valley, north of Adelaide! Even in Australia, the Sangiovese won't completely shed its slightly surly style, but the gentle strawberry fruit and teasing, nipping acidity make for a good drink.

2007 Côtes de Provence, MiP – Made in Provence, Domaine Sainte Lucie, Provence, France, 12% ABV
Lea and Sandeman, £8.95

I know they say that since most Côtes de Provence rosé is drunk ice-shard cold by broiling Brits on the Riviera strand it doesn't have to taste of anything. Hey, I've said it too. But Provence *can* be so much better than that – and this one shows how. A pale but fresh pink colour; bright, soft apple and anis smell; a lovely, almost memorable flavour of apple and pear flesh; lemon acidity; and a refreshing seasoning of fennel and mint.

2007 Malbec Rosé, Altosur, Finca Sophenia, Tupungato-Mendoza, Argentina, 12.5% ABV
Majestic Wine, £7.49

The pink that wants to be a red. The colour's pretty full, and the flavour is quite deep, halfway to red – it even has a slight nip of tannin. Whenever the Argentines make Malbec, they can't get the vision of a big juicy steak – sizzling on the barbie, bawling for red – out of their minds.

2007 Coteaux du Languedoc, Nord Sud, Laurent Miquel, Languedoc, France, 12.5% ABV
Tesco, £7.19

Properly dry, but with loads of fruit. Fresh, mouthwatering stuff, piled high with soft, pink strawberry flesh and the dripping juiciness of pears.

2007 Beaujolais Rosé, Domaine de Grandmont, France, 12.5% ABV
Christopher Piper, £6.99

I'm sufficiently keen on real *red* Beaujolais that I can feel slightly cheated when it turns up as pink. But I like this one, with its pale salmon colour, a fresh scent of apple blossom and dry summer earth, and a full, fleshy flavour, dry but juicy, apple and ripe red plum married with the softness of a breakfast brioche.

2007 Mâcon Rosé (Cave de Prissé), Burgundy, France, 12.5% ABV
Marks & Spencer, £6.99

I know rosé's not supposed to be serious, but this is vaguely on the serious side: although it has attractive strawberry and apple fruit, it *is* pretty dry and the dryness is accentuated by the rub of stones and a refreshing streak of metal.

2007 Slowine Rosé, WO Overberg, South Africa, 12.5% ABV Flagship Wines, £6.99

An arresting bright cherry pink colour – I'd have expected a Slowine to be rather less energizing in appearance – but the flavour is calmer: gentle, round, slightly fat but in a chubby, comforting way, comforting like a crumble of apple and strawberry, lightly splashed with cream.

2007 Pinot Grigio Superiore, Ramato, Breganze, Cantina Beato Bartolomeo da Breganze, Veneto, Italy, 12.5% ABV Majestic Wine, £6.49

Pinot Grigio pink? Well, I suppose when you come to think of it, that shouldn't be such a shock: the Pinot is called 'Grigio' because the grapes go greyish-pink when they're ripe. And anyway, Pinot Grigio has become such a catch-all name nowadays, being pink is the least of its problems. What's more, this is rather nice, with a flavour of melons, a slight rasp of peach skins and tangy acidity. Colour? Ah, I forgot to take note.

2007 Merlot Rosé, Reserve Selection, Ormer Bay, Fairtrade, Western Cape, South Africa, 12% ABV Friarwood, £6.15

Most South African pinks have a mild creaminess to them, and this is no exception. The fruit is soft and ripe, apples and mellow strawberries, and the texture is soft and gentle. Cool it right down and enjoy.

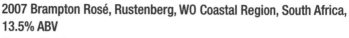

2007 Brampton Rosé, Rustenberg, WO Coastal Region, South Africa, 13.5% ABV
Co-op, £5.99

Rustenberg is one of South Africa's most reliable producers of really tasty wines: Brampton is the value-for-money range, but it doesn't skimp on flavour. This is full and soft, with a hint of leathery mellowness and even a whiff of toast, but the basic style is ripe, syrupy strawberries polished with the dryness of rocks and a sprinkling of herbs.

2007 Coteaux du Languedoc, Mescladis, Domaine Clavel, Languedoc, France, 13% ABV
The Wine Society, £5.95

As soon as I opened the bottle, the smell flooded out – most unexpected in a rosé! A beautiful mixture of softness with ripeness, the strawberry fruit is the kind that makes the fridge smell for days, the pear flesh so juicy you can sense it dripping down your chin.

2007 Côtes du Rhône Rosé, Cuvée Prestige, Sainsbury's (Les Vignerons de l'Enclave des Papes), Rhône Valley, France, 13.5% ABV
Sainsbury's, £4.99

Best-value pink I've come across this year: real Rhône character for not a lot of money. It's bright, it's fresh, quite fleshy and able to mix the juiciness of apple and strawberry with an austere edge from the stony vineyards of the southern Rhône Valley.

2007 Merlot Rosé, Los Robles, Fairtrade, Curicó Valley, Chile, 13.5% ABV
Booths, £4.99, Sainsbury's, £5.19

Los Robles in Chile have been making tremendous, crunchy Fairtrade reds for a few years now, so I'm delighted to see them coming up with a really tasty pink: rich and round, almost plummy, but with nice, leafy acidity. If you think it's not quite dry, it's the quality of that Chilean fruit shining through. Just leave it in the fridge for another hour.

2007 Languedoc Rosé, Vin de Pays d'Oc, Extra Special (JC Mas), Languedoc, France, 13% ABV
Asda, £4.62

Jean Claude Mas is one of France's most up-to-date and unfussy guys – he self-deprecatingly invented the Arrogant Frog brand. This is a typical crowd-pleaser, with mild pear and raspberry fruit and a gentle, winning, creamy texture.

2006 Vin de Pays des Côtes de Gascogne, Harmonie de Gascogne, Domaine de Pellehaut, South-West France, 12% ABV
Booths, £4.49

Domaine de Pellehaut is one of Gascony's best individual white wine producers, so it's delightful to find that it's a dab hand at rosé too. The flavour really does reflect the cool South-West of France – the slightly tousled autumn taste of windfall apples and the rasp of plum skins, but with an enjoyable squashy texture sharpened up by the tang of blackcurrant leaves and the chewiness of apple core.

Keeping it light

We're becoming increasingly disenchanted with high-alcohol wines. So, increasingly, I'm checking the alcohol content of the wines I recommend. Here are my suggestions for drinks with fab flavours that won't leave you fuzzy-headed the next morning.

More and more wines seem to be hitting our shores at 14%, 15% – a couple of wines in this year's tastings came in at 16%. Red table wines! How can you enjoy that as a jolly beverage to knock back with your lamb chops: you'll be asleep or drunk before you've got the meat off the barbie.

Now, some wines have traditionally been high alcohol, and wear their strength well, but there are far too many wines that – less than a decade ago – used to perform at 11.5–12.5% alcohol and which are now adding at least a degree – and often more – to their strength, seemingly in an effort to ape the ripe round flavours of the New World. Thank goodness there are still a significant number showing more restraint.

At 12.5% there are lots of wines, particularly from cooler parts of France – most Beaujolais is 12–12.5% – northern Italy, where the most famous examples would be the Veneto reds Valpolicella and Bardolino and the white Soave, and from numerous parts of Eastern Europe, particularly Hungary.

But we've set the bar at 12%. This cuts out a lot of red wines; the slightly tart, refreshing white styles that sit easily at 12% can develop better flavour at a lower strength than most reds can. This exercise reminded us that Germany is full of fantastic Riesling wines as low as 7.5%. Muscadet is usually only 12%. Most supermarket house reds and whites are 11.5–12%. Western Australian whites are often 12%. And Champagne, of all things, is only 12%. Hallelujah.

White wine

- 2006 Bacchus, Chapel Down, Kent, England, £9.49, Waitrose, 11.5% ABV (page 46)
- 2006 Bordeaux Blanc, Château Le Grand Verdus, France, £9.90, Friarwood, 12% ABV (page 45)
- 2006 Bordeaux, Châteaux Selection, France, £3.49, Aldi, 12% ABV
- 2007 Bordeaux Sauvignon, Dourthe No 1, £6.99, Waitrose, 12% ABV
- 2007 Chenin Blanc, Peter Lehmann, Barossa, South Australia, £6.49, Waitrose, 11.5% ABV
- 2006 Chenin-Chardonnay, Vin de Pays des Côtes de Gascogne, Domaine du Tariquet, South-West France, £4.89, Booths, 12% ABV (page 86)
- 2007 Colombard-Sauvignon Blanc, La Biondina, Primo Estate, McLaren Vale, South Australia, £8.50, Australian Wine Centre, 12% ABV
- 2006 Colombard-Ugni Blanc, Vin de Pays des Côtes de Gascogne, Beaulieu, South-West France, £5.95, Savage Selection, 11.5% ABV (page 84)
- 2007 Vin de Pays des Côtes de Gascogne, la Courtine, Producteurs Plaimont, South-West France, £5.70, Christopher Piper, 11.5% ABV (page 84)
- 2006 Vin de Pays des Côtes de Gascogne, Domaine de Pellehaut, South-West France, £4.49, Booths, 12% ABV (page 86)
- 2007 Cuvée Pêcheur, Vin de Pays du Comté Tolosan, South-West France, £3.69, Waitrose, 11.5% ABV
- 2007 Cuvée de Richard, Vin de Pays du Comté Tolosan, South-West France, £3.79, Majestic, 11.5% ABV
- 2007 Furmint, Verus Vineyards, Ormoz, Slovenia, £7.99, The Real Wine Company, 12% ABV (page 52)
- 2007 Grand Héron, Vin de Pays des Côtes de Gascogne, South-West France, £4.99, Majestic, 11.5% ABV
- 2006 Gringet, Les Alpes, Vin de Savoie, D & P Belluard, France, £12.90, les Caves de Pyrene, 12% ABV (page 35)
- 2007 Moulin de Gassac, Vin de Pays de l'Hérault, Mas de Daumas Gassac, Languedoc-Roussillon, France, £5.99, Averys, 12% ABV
- 2007 Muscadet Côtes de Grandlieu Sur Lie, Fief Guérin, Loire Valley, France, £5.49, Waitrose, 12% ABV
- 2007 Muscadet Sèvre et Maine Sur Lie, Taste the Difference, Loire Valley, France, £4.99, Sainsbury's, 12% ABV (page 85)
- 2007 Muscadet Sèvre et Maine Sur Lie, Domaine de la Tourmaline, Loire Valley, France, £5.99, Majestic, 12% ABV
- 2006 Petit Chablis, Domaine d'Elise, Burgundy, France, Stone, Vine & Sun, £8.75. 12% ABV
- 2006 Pinot Blanc, Mise du Printemps, Josmeyer, Alsace, France, £9.99, Booths, 12% ABV
- 2007 Poacher's Blend, St Hallett, Barossa, South Australia, £6.99, Tesco, 12% ABV

- 2007 Riesling, Tim Adams, Clare Valley, South Australia, £9.20, Australian Wine Centre, Tesco, 12% ABV (page 47)
- 2007 Riesling, Basserman-Jordan, Pfalz, Germany, £7.99, Waitrose, 10.5% ABV
- 2006 Riesling, Blue Slate, Dr Loosen, Mosel, Germany, about £8, Flagship Wines, Somerfield, 8% ABV (page 52)
- 2007 Riesling, Eldredge Vineyards, Clare Valley, South Australia, £8.99, Australian Wine Centre, 12% ABV (page 48)
- 2006 Riesling, Grafenreben, Alsace, France, £7.99, Waitrose, 12% ABV
- 2004 Riesling Kabinett, Trierer Deutschherrenberg, Deutschherrenhof, Mosel, Germany, £5.99, Majestic, 8% ABV (page 83)
- 2006 Riesling Kabinett, Piesporter Goldtröpfchen, Kurt Hain, Mosel, Germany, £9.50, Tanners, 8% ABV (page 45)
- 2006 Riesling Kabinett, Ürziger Würzgarten, Dr Loosen, Mosel, Germany, £11.99, Waitrose, 8% ABV (page 39)
- 2006 Riesling, Harewood Estate, Denmark, Great Southern, Western Australia, £9.95, Great Western Wine, 11.5% ABV
- 2007 Riesling, Opou Vineyard, Millton, Gisborne, New Zealand, £10.99, Vintage Roots, 9% ABV
- 2006 Riesling, Steillage, Mosel, Germany, £6.19, Tesco Finest, 11% ABV (page 82)
- 2006 Riesling, Terrassen, Huber, Traisental, Austria, £9.99, Oddbins, 12% ABV
- 2007 Rioja, Gran Familia, Bodegas Castillo de Fuenmayor, Rioja, Spain, £5.49, Co-op, 12% ABV
- 2007 Sauvignon Blanc, Oxford Landing, South Australia, £7.49, widely available, 11.5% ABV
- 2007 Semillon, Brokenwood, Hunter Valley, New South Wales, Australia, £10.49, Liberty Wines, 11.5% ABV (page 42)
- 2007 Semillon, Denman Vineyard, Hunter Valley, New South Wales, Australia, £6.99, Tesco Finest, 10.5% ABV (page 58)
- 2002 Semillon, Mount Pleasant Elizabeth, McWilliam's, Hunter Valley, New South Wales, Australia, £13.99, Philglas & Swiggot, 10.5% ABV
- 2006 Soave Classico, Italy, £3.48, Asda, 12% ABV
- 2007 Vieille Fontaine, Vin de Pays du Gers, South-West France, £3.40, Tesco, 11.5% ABV (page 97)
- 2007 Villa Antinori, Tuscany, Italy, £7.99, Morrisons, Tanners, 12% ABV (page 55)
- 2007 Viña Sol, Torres, Penedes, Cataluna, Spain, £5.99, widely available, 11.5% ABV
- 2007 Vinho Verde, Quinta de Azevedo, Portugal, £5.99, Majestic, Waitrose, 11% ABV (page 83)
- 1990 Vouvray, Aigle Blanc, Prince Poniatowski, Loire Valley France, £11.00, Waterloo Wine, 12% ABV (page 39)

Rosé wine

- 2007 Bordeaux Rosé, Château Bel Air, France, £6.95, The Wine Society, 12% ABV
- 2007 Chapel Down rosé, England, £8.99, Waitrose, 11.5% ABV
- 2005 Cheverny, Domaine Sauger, Loire Valley, France, £8.99, Flagship Wines, 12% ABV
- 2007 Côtes de Provence, MiP, Domaine Sainte Lucie, Provence, France, £8.95, Lea and Sandeman, 12% ABV (page 103)
- 2007 Le Froglet Rosé, Vin de Pays d'Oc, Languedoc, France, £4.49, Marks & Spencer, 12% ABV
- 2007 Merlot Rosé, Ormer Bay, South Africa, £6.15, Friarwood, 12% ABV (page 105)
- 2007 Rioja Rosado, Gran Familia, Bodegas Castillo de Fuenmayor, Rioja, Spain, £5.19, Tesco, 12% ABV
- 2006 Vin de Pays des Côtes de Gascogne, Domaine de Pellehaut, South-West France, £4.49, Booths, 12% ABV (page 107)
- 2007 Zwelgelt Rosé, Hesperia, Felsner, Austria, £7.19, Waitrose, 11.5% ABV

Red wine

- 2006 Beaujolais, France, £3.76, Asda, 12% ABV (page 100)
- 2006 Beaujolais, Cuvée Terroir, Domaine Chatelus, Beaujolais, France, £7.55, Roger Harris Wines, 12% ABV
- 2005 Carso, Terrano, Zidarich, Friuli-Venezia Giulia, Italy, £20.60, Les Caves de Pyrene, 11.5% ABV (page 32)
- 2006 Cuvée Chasseur, Vin de Pays de l'Hérault, Languedoc-Roussillon, France, £3.29, Waitrose, 12% ABV (page 101)
- Cuvée de Richard, Vin de Pays de l'Aude, Languedoc-Roussillon, France, £3.79, Majestic, 12% ABV
- 2007 House Wine, Vin de Pays du Comté Tolosan, South-West France, £3.49, Marks & Spencer, 12% ABV
- 2007 Syrah, Vin de Pays de l'Ardèche, Cave Saint-Désirat, Rhône Valley, France, £4.49, Booths, 12% ABV (page 93)
- 2007 Teroldego delle Venezie, Novello delle Viviene, Italy, £7.39, Laithwaites, 12% ABV (page 74)
- 2007 Trinacria Rosso, Sicily, Italy, £3.60, Waitrose, 12% ABV
- 2007 Vieille Fontaine, Vin de Pays du Comté Tolosan, South-West France, £3.40, Tesco, 12% ABV

FIZZ

You can never count the Champagne producers out. Just as the large brands began to see their growth start to stutter – and in the case of one or two *very* big brands like Moët, volumes actually fell last year – just as my tastings of the famous labels had me shaking my head at the dumbing down of flavours, just as I'm about to beat the drum for Champagne-method sparkling wine from elsewhere in France, Spain, New Zealand, South Africa – and say 'save your money, this'll do fine' – I begin to notice a perceptible improvement in the quality of Champagne on our shelves and, with a few honourable exceptions, a decline in the quality of non-Champagne sparkling wines. Bah! I was going to rail against the Champagne producers' drive to expand their vineyards, saying it's just greed, and now I taste a wide range of relatively cheap Champagnes, many from lesser vineyard zones, and find myself smiling at their style and taste and value for money. Maybe those vineyard expansions will help rather than hinder us fizz drinkers. And maybe they will serve to remind the world's other fizz producers that the only way they'll be able to fight Champagne is to relentlessly keep the quality up. This year has seen non-Champagne sales go up and quality go down. That smacks of short-term gain and long-term stupidity.

• The wines are listed in descending price order.

2005 Balfour Brut Rosé, Kent, England, 12.5% ABV
Bibendum, £33.00

A new entrant into the top British fizz arena. So far, this Kentish producer has been famous for producing some of the country's best apple juice, at the Hush Heath Estate, near Cranbrook. But Richard Balfour-Lynn makes classy fizz too: very pale orange pink, attractively acidic in style, with a scent of honeysuckle and fresh leather and a flavour of soft dry cream and apples rubbed with smooth stones.

nv Champagne, Blanc de Blancs Brut, Delamotte, France, 12% ABV
Corney & Barrow, £29.99

Here's an example of superb base material really making the difference. This is Chardonnay-only wine, and the grapes were grown in Le Mesnil, which, if I had to choose, I just might plump for as my favourite Champagne village of all. This is a little young still, beautifully frothy and pure in the mouth, but if you hang on to it for 6–12 months more, the dry apple fruit and pale creaminess will deepen and become sweetened with cream fudge and flecked with honey.

nv Champagne, Brut Tradition Grand Cru, Ambonnay, Egly-Ouriet, France, 12.5% ABV Lea and Sandeman, £29.95

Marvellous old-fashioned stuff. Don't waste this on some thirsty dude you've just met in a bar. Keep it for friends trusted and true, because it's quite an experience. Champagne gets its sparkle from a second fermentation in the bottle. The yeast sediment is usually removed after a year or two, at most, but this bubbly stayed sitting on that tasty, creamy yeast for 38 months, and given that the grapes came from the powerhouse village of Ambonnay, the result is an austere and impressive mouthful of apple flesh, brown and slightly bruised, rice krispies cereal softness and a gaunt, shining, hazelnut husk dryness.

nv Champagne, Brut Zero, Tarlant, France, 12% ABV
Marks & Spencer, £25

And now for something completely different. Champagne is made from very acid grapes so, just before they ram the final cork in the bottle, the producers add a little sugar to neutralize the acidity and soften things up. But this one is a 'Brut Zero', which means they didn't add any sugar to help the flavour out. So they must have been very confident of their grapes. Well, it helps when you're a grower who's been producing grapes in the attractive little village of Oeuilly, just west of Epernay, since 1687. You've sort of got the hang of your vines by now. It's also encouraging to find a big operation like M&S prepared to take a punt on a single-producer wine. Most Champagnes are blends made up by big companies or co-operatives. But more and more growers are gaining the confidence to produce their own stuff, and if you like Champagne full of flavour and personality, with the rough edges and quirks not smoothed away, then grower Champagne is for you. Like this one: the acidity is high – but only like it's high in a good Chablis – there's a spicy softness, attractive balanced apple fruit and a certain nut husk dryness. It proves that if the base material is good enough and you're prepared to spend a bit of time and effort aging the wine, you don't need to add sugar.

nv Champagne, De Brissar, France, 12% ABV
Threshers, Wine Rack, £24.99

Own-label Champagnes don't usually have the lovely yeasty softness that marks out the classy labels – either for reasons of cost-cutting or laziness. But this one is good. It's spent quite a long time in contact with its yeast, which gives it its creamy roundness, and also has a pleasant flavour of loft apples and the gentleness of hazelnuts.

nv Champagne, Premier Cru, Blanc de Blancs Brut, De Saint Gall, France, 12% ABV Marks & Spencer, £23.99

Lovely, mellow fizz made entirely from white Chardonnay grapes – and it comes from the best large-scale supplier of Chardonnay grapes in Champagne, the co-operative at Avize. Once again, well done M&S for taking fizz seriously. This isn't cheap for a supermarket own-label, but just taste the gentle apple flesh fruit, the soft hazelnut and milk chocolate and the creamy foam, and I think you'll be convinced.

2003 Vintage Champagne, Premier Cru, Duval-Leroy, France, 12.5% ABV Sainsbury's Taste the Difference, £23.99

Most of Duval-Leroy's Champagne is rather anonymous stuff, but in 2003, a drought year when a lot of Champagne producers struggled to produce anything half decent, Duval-Leroy made a very good stab at it. This is full, quite chunky, but juicy too, with a broad, creamy, yeast feel and just a whiff of freshly toasted white bread.

nv Champagne, Premier Cru, Pierre Vaudon, France, 12% ABV
Haynes Hanson & Clark, £22.60

My favourite fizz from this year's tastings. This is one of those
Champagnes that you get at smart parties. You have a glass.
Mmm, that's good, I wonder what it is? And over the years the host has probably revealed a bottle of Pierre
Vaudon more often than any other. It's the creaminess, the gentleness of the foam, the hint of fudge and the
suggestion of shortbread that make it such an excellent drink. It's made by a large co-operative, but it's the
Avize co-op, and Avize is one of Champagne's top villages. I suspect Pierre Vaudon is one of their top cuvées.

nv Champagne, Premier Cru, Rilly La Montagne, Philippe Brugnon, France, 12% ABV
The Oxford Wine Company, £20.95

This comes as a bit of a shock, because it doesn't really
taste like Champagne at all. Yet it *is* a good drink and I'd
happily spend a party downing it. In a way it has too much
fruit – a high-toned, scented jumble of apple sauce and pear
flesh with added pudding spice and a splash of cream. Too
much fruit for Champagne? We should be grateful. The usual problem is not enough.

nv Champagne, Blanc de Blancs Brut (P&C Heidsieck), France, 12% ABV   Waitrose, £19.99

This is made for Waitrose by Charles Heidsieck, the classiest of the big Champagne houses, and is a
stunningly reliable fizz. It always has a softness of milk chocolate and cream – almost as though someone
has sprinkled cocoa dust in the glass – as well as a gently reviving acidity and fresh fluffy apple fruit.

nv Champagne, Cuvée Brut, Oudinot, France, 12% ABV
Marks & Spencer, £19.99

Oudinot is M&S's mainstream Champagne brand. If it seems expensive, by all means shop elsewhere, but I taste these own-labels against each other and I have no hesitation in saying that M&S deliver. This has far more personality than most other High Street own-labels, with its soft, yeasty smell, its beautifully judged, foaming, caressing bubbles and its flavour like part-baked Bramley apples, touched by coriander seed spice and dabbed with whipped cream and icing sugar.

2005 Bloomsbury, Ridgeview, West Sussex, England, 12% ABV
£18–£20, Waitrose, The Wine Society, The English Wine Centre, Alfriston, East Sussex (www.englishwine.co.uk), Butler's Wine Cellars and other independent retailers

Ridgeview has done as much as anyone to take English fizz on to another level. It has plugged away at proving that Sussex is as good a place as Champagne for growing the Champagne grapes and making a very Champagne-like wine. This has a lovely foaming mousse, fairly evident but integrated acidity, and a full, round flavour of fresh apples and cream, a suggestion of strawberries and more than a suggestion of hedgerow scent. In 2–3 years this 2005 will have a richness like toffee cream. If you can wait.

2004 English Sparkling Wine Rosé, Chapel Down, Kent, England, 12% ABV
Sainsbury's Taste the Difference, £17.99

The English are on the march. English fizz is not only being taken seriously, it's selling out. Queues are forming, scuffles are breaking out and handbags being aimed. Has the world gone mad? Well, no. England has got fantastic conditions for growing the light, fragrant, rather acid grapes that make the best Champagne – sorry, sparkling wine. Some British bubbly resembles good Champagne, but this one is unmistakably English: very pale pink in colour, redolent of hedgerows and underripe late summer pears, with the sappiness of spring twigs and a little rosehip syrup richness mixed with cream.

nv Crémant de Bourgogne, Grande Reserve, Perle de Vigne, Louis Bouillot, Burgundy, France, 12% ABV
Majestic Wine, £11.99

For years, sparkling Burgundy has been a stalwart of those who want Champagne flavours but don't want to pay Champagne prices. Sometimes the wines are virtually indistinguishable. This one doesn't taste quite like Champagne – it has good apple flesh fruit and nutty softness, but also quite a bit of spice as well as a slightly leafy tang – but it's a good drink.

nv Jansz Rosé, Yalumba, Tasmania, Australia, 12% ABV
Oddbins, £11.49

I only discovered this a year ago and I seem to have downed a ridiculous amount of it since then. It is delightful stuff – very pale salmon pink, a cascade of bubbles that foams helter-skelter around your mouth and up into your brain, and a mild, mellow flavour of apples, strawberries and cream.

nv Prosecco di Conegliano-Valdobbiadene, La Marca, Veneto, Italy, 11% ABV
Majestic Wine, £10.49

Prosecco has become extremely popular for its soft fruit flavour and gentle bubble, but I'm disappointed by the general standard on the High Street. They're not fresh enough – and freshness is everything with Prosecco. Well, this one *is* fresh: it has a lovely, bright, simple flavour of apples and pears, a foaming mouthful of bubbles and a hint of syrup richness – which is very nice, so long as the wine is fresh.

2005 Cava Vintage Brut, Spain, 11.5% ABV
Marks & Spencer, £8.99

Some of you may balk at paying £8.99 for an own-label Cava – but M&S do take their fizz very seriously. This has a lot of flavour and much more fruit than a typical non-vintage Cava. The acidity is quite strong, but there's a good dose of green apple juice, a splash of syrupy richness and a good cream and hazelnut aftertaste to keep you happy.

2005 Crémant de Limoux, Cuvée Saint Laurent, Georges et Roger Antech, Languedoc, France, 12% ABV
The Wine Society, £7.50

Before the New World, before Spanish Cava even, there was a dependable, affordable, good-quality sparkler from South-West France called Blanquette de Limoux. It was based on the Mauzac grape and always had quite a sharp taste of green apples. I suppose you might say you had to get used to it. So the Limoux authorities decided to make things easier for us poor fizz enthusiasts and planted the quicker-ripening Chardonnay and Chenin varieties to facilitate production of a more 'internationalist' type of bubbly. And here it is. Gentle, quite full, with a nice bubble and a flavour of lightly bruised apples, nuts and confectioner's cream. Very nice. Quite like rather a lot of other fizzes, though.

nv Gotas de Plata Rosé, Viñedos y Reservas, La Mancha, Spain, 11.5% ABV Adnams, £7.50

Hey, this is fun. It's from Spain, where most decent fizz is called Cava, but clearly these guys, lost in the wilds to the south of Madrid, aren't allowed, so they call it 'Metodo Tradicional'. And I've never seen a Cava quite this pink. I've *certainly* never seen a Champagne half as pink. The flavour doesn't let you down: it's a real blast of strawberry jam and apple flesh fruit, almost too much of a good thing, but drink it really cold and it's a blast. A rock festival, an ice box and a few of these. That's the way to do it.

nv Cava Brut, Vineyard X, Covides, Spain, 11.5% ABV
Threshers, Wine Rack, £5.99 (3 for 2, £3.99)

Brilliant party wine. It's fresh, it's got good acidity and a touch of perfume, as well as quite full apple syrup fruit and an acceptable earthy finish. Chill it right down and turn the music up.

nv Cava Rosé Brut, Spain, 12% ABV Somerfield, £5.09

Somerfield's pink Cava is as good as ever. And as pink. It's never been a shy retiring little petal of a thing – it packs loads of strawberry fruit, even a touch of syrupy richness and icing sugar softness, but the fresh acidity is there and so is a good stony rasp that stops it tasting too rich.

nv Cava Rosado Brut, Mas Miralda, Penedès, Spain, 11.5% ABV Asda, £3.98

Asda has some good things at bargain-basement prices, and this is no exception. It's pale salmon pink, with a reasonable pink fruit flavour sharpened up with a little pepper and blackcurrant leaf before a touch of earth intrudes. Chill it down and approach it in party mood.

SWEETIES

I've read it more than once this year: 'sweet wines are not of our time'. And I can sympathize with the writers. Sweet wines – truly sweet wines, not just mildly sweet commercial plonk from Germany or California or Australia – take time to appreciate. That sounds silly. Sugar takes no time at all to appreciate: a child can appreciate it in a split second. But real, traditional sweet wines do not just taste of sugar; they have a fascinating and sometimes bewildering range of flavours which are created by very special and labour-intensive methods of overripening the grapes and fermenting them so that the essence of the grape's character is preserved, not just the sugar sweetness. It's not easy, it's not cheap, and few regions in the whole world achieve it. But sit back, close your eyes and let these lovely liquids flow around your mouth as the cares of the day recede, and you'll realize that simply to swig them back is a dreadful waste. The Italians call such wines 'wines of contemplation'. That's the mood I'm in when I open a bottle.

• The wines are listed in descending price order.

2004 Recioto di Soave, Vigna Marogne, Tamellini, Veneto, Italy, 13.5% ABV
Les Caves de Pyrène, £20.00/500ml

Trust Caves de Pyrène to come up with the most absorbing, challenging sweet wine I've had this year. Caves de Pyrène only deal in challenging wines. If you're up for it, you'll find their details on page 163. Soave is usually a simple dry white, frequently of no personality whatsoever. But it can be a great dry white, and it first made its reputation, 1500 years ago, as a *sweet* wine. You don't see the sweet wine around much because it's very difficult to make and involves complicated selection of grapes, semi-drying of the bunches after harvest and very tricky fermentation. And at the end you get a beautiful wild child like this. Dayglo gold hinting at orange, and flavours that I defy you to find in any other wine. For a start, it's sweet, but it's also tannic, rich and rough, mixing the juice of pomegranates and the flesh of quince, papaya, Alphonso mangos and guava, with the pomegranate seeds and the rough fibres and skins of these tropical fruits. The sweetness of the flesh right next to the skins, the bitterness of the fibres and seeds, and just to turn things right on their head, the half-forgotten sugar-starch vegetable richness of Carrots Vichy à la Elizabeth David c. 1955.

2006 Alicante, Moscatel, Casta Diva, Cosecha Miel, Bodegas Gutiérrez de la Vega, Spain, 13.5% ABV
Direct Wine Shipments, £14.99/500ml

This is one of those wines I go back to again and again, searching for the precise flavours until suddenly the bottle's empty and my notes still make no sense. Ah well, bear with me, because this is good. I start out OK – this is a rich but slightly strange mix of muscatel syrup and honey, leather and toasty smoke, green Meltis fruit and spearmint chews – oops, here I go. Well, after that I bounce between russet apple juice – russet, mind you – cloudy and just starting to go stale, and baked peach jam on a tart. Mmm, now I'm drifting.

Something reminds me of my first skiing holiday in Austria aged 18: the gluhwein? The ski-wax? The pheromones? And now it's the tonic drink you get for breakfast at the Grand Hotel in Stockholm. All right, I'll come quietly.

2005 Scheurebe Beerenauslese, Dürkheimer Spielberg, Darting Estate, Pfalz, Germany, 9.5% ABV
Marks & Spencer, £13.99/50cl

Scheurebe's not a well-known grape, but in the southern Rhine Valley it produces spectacular grapefruit- and honey-flavoured sweet wines. This is impressive stuff. The grapefruit and honey have had cling peach syrup poured in too, and someone dripping fresh athletic sweat has mashed in some green stem ginger to give it extra spice and feral allure.

2006 Ultime Récolte, Jeff Carrel, France, 13% ABV
The Real Wine Company, £12.00

The name means 'the last harvest, the late grapes, the moment before they literally fell off the vine because they were so oozing with sugar and ripeness'. Well, that's how I interpret it – and so does winemaker Jeff Carrel, but he can't explain it to us on the label because he's broken certain idiotic French laws to make the wine, so he can only call it Vin de Table, table wine, the lowest of the low, no details allowed. So forget the label, taste the wine. It's absolutely delicious: full and rich but marvellously fresh and not over-sweet – juicy yellow peach flesh and pineapple, dusted with cinnamon and ginger and the skin of a really ripe Cox's apple left marinating in the vat to keep the liquid fresh. In South-West France they produce a style of sweet wine they call 'aperitif', which is not quite as rich as the after-dinner type. This is an excellent example.

nv Fine Old Muscat, Buller, Victoria, Australia, 18% ABV
Majestic Wine, £10.99

To be honest, I don't think it's possible to find a bad Australian Liqueur Muscat. These Muscats are made up in the old goldfields of north-east Victoria. The grapes are left to shrivel in the vineyards and then they're picked, crushed and thrown into the vat. And virtually before they've had a chance to start fermenting, they're stunned into a petrified state of sweetness by the addition of high-alcohol spirit, which stops the fermentation ever getting going. So they're not really fortified wines, they're just fantastic mouthfuls of grape essence, aged in small barrels under the heat of the Australian sun until they achieve a burnished brilliance of brownness. It's so deep and rich it almost hurts your teeth, it's a lush goo of fig biscuits, old raisins and sultanas, spinster aunt's dates (perhaps I should rephrase that) and all those strange brown things that go into Christmas puddings and are best left unidentified.

2007 Weisser Riesling Noble Late Harvest, Paul Cluver, WO Elgin, South Africa, 12% ABV
Christopher Piper Wines, £8.99/half bottle

This comes from a high, cool, damp mountain pass. The cloud often hangs over the vines for days on end during summer. This won't help ripen a Shiraz, but it will keep the acid in white grapes high and encourage a little sugar-concentrating 'noble rot' late in the ripening season. The result is a wine not massively sweet, but with good fragrant honey mixed with apple syrup, an attractive bitter grapefruit zest nip and a certain rough rub of stones.

2003 Jurançon, Chamarré Tradition, South-West France, 12.5% ABV Co-op, £7.99

Jurançon is rarely fantastically sweet; in fact its strength is its gutsy blend of pineapple with acidity, sweet tropical fruit cut through with lemon juice and green apple peel. Well, that's what you get here – the pineapple recruits some honey and quince, the apples are lightly baked and the lemon has been squeezed on to a ripe tomato. Hmm. No wonder they usually drink Jurançon with the first course or with cheese.

2006 Cantavida, Late Harvest, Single Vineyard, Limarí Valley, Chile, AF Arco Iris, 14% ABV
Oddbins, £6.89/50cl

A new departure for Chile: high-quality sweet wine. This is a mix of Muscat and Viognier grapes grown in virtual desert, way north of Santiago. That doesn't sound promising, but I've visited Limarí – the fierce coastal winds keep the temperature right down, and the vineyards and winery are 'state of the art'. Just like this wine. Modern, fresh, rich, lovely apricot and pineapple sweetness, some grapiness from the Muscat, some superripe grapefruit and peach-skin rasp, and an exotic sprinkling of cinnamon and clove.

2007 Orange Muscat & Flora, Brown Brothers, Victoria, Australia, 9.5% ABV
Somerfield, £6.49/half bottle

This is a dinner party standby, the old faithful to go with the crème brûlée or the tiramisu. Well, you could serve it thus, though I'd prefer it with fruit, nuts and blue cheese. You could just as well serve it ice cold as an aperitif or even with a first course – Roquefort and walnut salad? Foie gras? It is a very reliable wine, and this year it's better than ever: bright, sweet, easy-going, apple blossom scent mixed with blood orange juice, honey and grape richness, and a mild come-hither acidity as subtle as the flesh of a Golden Delicious.

nv Moscatel de Valencia, Spain, 15% ABV Asda, £3.28

This isn't really wine at all. It's superripe grape juice fortified with high-strength spirit – but do I care? No. It's a fantastically reliable wodge of fat, luscious, juicy sweetness. Grape juice and honey sharpened just a little by green apple peel acidity and a streak of cold mineral. And I thought I noted some floral scent. At this price? Surely not.

FORTIFIED WINES

It would be a lot easier to write about sherry if we had more predictable weather. Finos and manzanillas for those long and lazy summer days, olorosos and amontillados for when the evenings draw in and the temperature drifts down to single figures. But as I gaze out of my window at what is supposed to be a glorious summer afternoon – and I'm wearing a sweater indoors and it's sheeting down outside, and I think back to February when the temperature sat happily around 20°C for day after day – it just becomes so difficult to say when you should drink sherry. A glass of chilled fino as a reward when I've finished this paragraph? Or a bumper of fiery port? But this may partly explain why fortified wine sales are not exactly healthy: we never seem to know when to drink them nowadays. Their traditional roles as pick-me-ups, aperitifs or post-prandial carousers have become blurred. Even so, they are some of the great classic wines of the world. Sherry does need a bit of an effort to understand, but is a deeply satisfying wine. Port is absurdly easy to enjoy – you don't *have* to understand it, but you'll get much more excitement out of it if you make the effort, and you'll get much more value for your money too.

- In this section you will find sherries first, then ports, in descending price order.

SHERRY

Oloroso Muy Viejo, Bodegas Tradición, 20% ABV
Fortnum & Mason, £18.50/half bottle

A pale tawny colour might imply a mellow wine. Don't be fooled. Just as 100%
black chocolate shocks you with its dryness, so does this. Its bitterness and
asperity rasps like tamarind skin. It really *is* quite shocking, but excellent too –
deep, dry, you have to peer way past its gaunt exterior to find a richness of nut and
chocolate, date and fig that is stripped and flayed of all sugar, all indulgence, all
mellowness and reassuring flesh. This is the Grand Inquisitor of sherries, this is the
great ascetic, the flagellator, the moaning, keening hermit of sherries. It is
magnificent, but you may have to drink it by yourself, wearing a hood.

Palo Cortado Muy Viejo/Very Old Palo Cortado, Apostoles, González Byass, 20% ABV
Fortnum & Mason, Harrods, House of Fraser, Sainsbury's (larger stores), £13.99/half bottle

To make any kind of sherry, even a light, dry fino such as Tio Pepe (see right), you need good stocks of older
sherries, since the core of sherry's character lies in the producer's ability to blend wines of all ages. Many
sherry houses have sold their birthright by running down these old 'soleras', as the stocks are called, for
short-term profit, and by doing so they have slammed the door against their chances of ever making great
sherry again. But González Byass keeps magnificent stocks, and uses them wisely and well. This Palo
Cortado is an almost dry sherry made up of wines averaging 30 years of age. It manages to be fat, and rich,
and acid, syrupy yet dry. Nut, raisin and sultana scent survive an onslaught of dense dried apricot and peach
flesh, a syrup that's scythed through by searing acidity, and a crumbly, cold dryness like wood ash in a
morning-after grate. I have a vision of a plate of pâté and cheese, made perfect by a glass of this.

Oloroso Dulce Viejo/Old Sweet Oloroso, Matusalem, González Byass, 20.5% ABV
Fortnum & Mason, Harrods, House of Fraser, Sainsbury's (larger stores),
£13.99/half bottle

This is great, warm wine, a mixture of power and lusciousness and age that only sherry can do. The wines used in this blend are all at least 30 years old, but there are elements far, far older than that. The label says It Is Old Sweet Oloroso. Well, it's old, but it's not that sweet – great sherries rarely are, even if the label says differently. But it *is* rich. Its deep amber brown colour carries on into the splendid dark flavour of baked dates, dried figs, raisins, prunes and black treacle all bound together with the appetizing twine of bitterness.

Fino Muy Seco, Tio Pepe, González Byass, 15% ABV
Most major retailers and supermarkets, £8.99

I see Tio Pepe quite regularly because I drink it nice and chilled in decent bars when I want something refreshing but just a little challenging – and it's been on form all year. I can see that they're trying to capture some of the white wine market, and they deserve to succeed. But it doesn't taste like Sauvignon or Pinot Grigio or Chardonnay. It's proudly, importantly different: a bready, sweet-sour yeasty smell, very dry fruit like the core of a green apple, a slight bitter rasp like tamarind skin, and the haunting, lonesome scent of time-bleached banisters in a clean and grand old house.

Manzanilla Pasada, Pastrana, Bodegas Hidalgo La Gitana, 15.5% ABV
The Wine Society, £8.95

For the first time in years I've recently found Hidalgo's mainstream La Gitana Manzanilla rather disappointing. Luckily this single-vineyard version of an aged manzanilla is on fine form. It's quite a deep green-gold, and has the sweet-sour bread yeast, green apple core and ancient banisters flavours of fine dry sherry, but in darker mood. Polished leather makes an appearance, brazil nuts and cream, and the kind of heady alcoholic fumes you'd find if you wandered through the great silent cellars where they store these wines.

Manzanilla Mariscal, 15% ABV Tanners, £8.80

A lady called Dolores Bustillo Delgado appears to make this. Understandably, I am impatient to visit such a paragon. However, no invitation wings its way from the Andalucian Atlantic shore. So I drink her wine and dream. It's a classic seaside manzanilla, very dry, but not rasping, full and bready with a definite sense of the savoury – is it sea salt or sausage, or Shippams meat paste? It's a little richer than it was a year or two ago – perhaps Dolores is too – but the refreshing, appetizing marriage of savoury with hazelnut husks, bread yeast, old wood and the lightest touch of ocean spray will do me for another year.

Fino del Puerto, Solera Jerezana, Waitrose/Emilio Lustau, 16.5% ABV Waitrose, £7.49

Many of the own-label dry sherries in our supermarkets at the moment are tasting of nothing very much, so thank goodness Waitrose hasn't given in to cost-cutting and dumbing down. This is £7.49 – some own-labels go as low as £3.99 – and it's 16.5% alcohol – most others are 15%. Consequently it has loads of character, the bread crust yeastiness married with an almost milky, nutty, soft bone-dryness, and the gaunt scent of dry old floorboards trailing through the wine and scouring your palate of sweet thoughts. Don't skimp on sherry. Pay for the good stuff.

Manzanilla, Las Medallas de Argüeso, 15% ABV
The Wine Society, £5.95

This is slightly old-fashioned – but I don't mind The Wine Society having a few old-fashioned wines. I'm sure they've got a few old-fashioned members who are absolutely delighted to drink them. But when I read my tasting notes and they start 'very savoury and Chuzzlewit', it does make me wonder – well, about my sanity for a start. Yet it *is* savoury, almost cheesily so, like a meat stock, but that goes fine with the twintered dried apple fruit and an unsugary richness like those nice brown bits from the bottom of a sponge cake tin. And then I find myself thinking of a spinster aunt's drawing room before Sunday lunch. And then a whiff of ether.

PORT

Graham's Crusted Port (bottled in 2001), 20% ABV
Sainsbury's, Thresher, £15.49

Graham's is one of the great old houses of port. It's now part of the Symington Group, which makes a lot of own-label port (on the whole, very well), but for the full glory of what Graham's can offer, you need to pay the extra for the label itself: the best barrels always go into the wine flying under its own colours. And this is splendid stuff. Crusted is a kind of semi-vintage port traditional to us Brits that was almost abolished a few

years ago, but furious opposition from these islands saved the style. Thank goodness. Because you get virtually vintage personality at half the price or less. This one has such fantastic purity, such balance, such mouthwatering fruit and succulence. The fresh blackberry and plum fruit coils and flirts with a fig and date richness, and a scent of herbs and mineral dust. Top drop.

2004 Niepoort LBV (bottled in 2008), 20% ABV
Ballantynes, Butlers Wine Cellar, Cambridge Wine Merchants, Great Northern Wines, Halifax Wine Company, Handford, Oxford Wine Company, Philglas & Swiggot, Tanners, £15.00

Most of the famous port houses were established by British families – but not all. The Dutch are important too, and the Niepoorts arrived in Oporto from the Netherlands in 1842. The wild and brilliant Dirk is the latest Niepoort to run the business, and he is one of Portugal's most exciting and innovative talents – for table wines as well as ports. This LBV is a shining example of his skills. Many modern LBVs (Late Bottled Vintages) are made industrially and are a good but not special drink. Niepoort takes an old-fashioned, non-interventionist approach, and comes up with a majestic example – sturdy and muscular with a fair splattering of pepper, tannin and stones, and spiritous power, but that's swamped by a laughing flood-tide of lush blackberry syrup, rosehip and violet scent and the acid-streaked sweetness of homemade damson jam.

10 year old Tawny Port, 20% ABV
Marks & Spencer, £12.99

You can get cheaper tawnies than this, but I wouldn't bother. Cheap tawny is usually a blend of red and white ports that nobody thought fit for drinking on their own. This wine is at least 10 years old – always look for a statement of age on tawnies – and the 10 years spent quietly aging in the barrels has mellowed and lightened the wine so it is now a burnished

amber colour, and its flavour is scented and soft – figs and dates and sultanas cosying up to brazil and hazelnut flesh and Christmas mincepies. This is *proper* tawny.

The Society's Exhibition Crusted Port (bottled in 2004), 20% ABV
The Wine Society, £12.50

Crusted port is a terrific style: all the flavour and excitement of vintage port, without quite the power. And this is seriously good value. The Wine Society is famous for the quality of its own-label ports and sherries – I suspect in the old days these made up the bulk of the Society's business. Well, the quality hasn't wavered in my memory. This is rich and scented, lush yet with a decent backbone of tannin and spirit. It has beautifully juicy loganberry and blackberry fruit steeped in syrup, swished with herbs and dusted with icing sugar. Drink it now, but it'll keep for a decade more.

2001 Late Bottled Vintage (bottled in 2007), Fonseca, 20% ABV
Majestic, £11.99

Superb value: Fonseca is one of the great names in port and this wine is unfiltered and un-mucked-about-with in the traditional, costly, time-consuming way. It's dark, deep wine, with some gentle pepper and spirit, a little herb too, but far more rich, lush black fruit – prunes and black plum and blackberry – nicely streaked with acidity and sprinkled with kitchen spice.

2001 Graham's Late Bottled Vintage Port (bottled in 2007), 20% ABV
Asda, Sainsbury's, Tesco, £11.99

Graham's quality shines through here. It's a dark, deep wine with a very direct quality to it – the flavour seems to focus right on the heart of your palate. It doesn't require understanding, just enjoying. That shouldn't be difficult. The wine has a lovely rich fruit of dark plums and blackberries, a refreshing acidity and lingering spice. Very easy to enjoy.

Reserve Port (organic), 20% ABV Marks & Spencer, £10.99

The name 'Reserve Port' doesn't mean anything, really, so you have to rely on the retailer's reputation. Luckily M&S's reputation for port is very good. They've gone to a 300-year-old family farm for this wine, a farm whose vines are organically grown – that's not too common with port – and they've come up with a delightful scented port that does have a bit of a pepper and spirit bite, but that merely acts as appetizing seasoning for the floral scents of peach and pear and the dark, rich, round, luscious fruit.

Pink Port, 19.5% ABV Marks & Spencer, £7.99/50cl

Think outside the box. If people aren't drinking port, if the 'yoof' market doesn't get it, break the rules, go wild. Pink is cool. Let's do pink. Never been a pink port before. Fine, we won't make this one look or taste

like any port before. I wasn't sure I could buy all that, but then I took a slug – ripe, soft strawberry, scented cherries and rosehip syrup, an apple flesh acidity. Pretty pretty pink, juicy Lucy fruit and cornerstore scent – hey, why not?

Storing, serving and tasting

Wine is all about enjoyment, so don't let anyone make you anxious about opening, serving, tasting and storing it. Here are some tips to help you enjoy your wine all the more.

The corkscrew

The first step in tasting any wine is to extract the cork. Look for a corkscrew with an open spiral and a comfortable handle. The Screwpull brand is far and away the best, with a high-quality open spiral. 'Waiter's friend' corkscrews – the type you see used in restaurants – are good too, once you get the knack.

Corkscrews with a solid core that looks like a giant woodscrew tend to mash up delicate corks or get stuck in tough ones. And try to avoid those 'butterfly' corkscrews with the twin lever arms and a bottle opener on the end; they tend to leave cork crumbs floating in the wine.

Corks

Don't be a cork snob. The only requirements for the seal on a bottle of wine are that it should be hygienic, airtight, long-lasting and removable. Real cork is environmentally friendly, but is prone to shrinkage and infection, which can taint the wine. Synthetic closures modelled on the traditional cork are common in budget wines, but the largest increase has been in the use of screwcaps, or Stelvin closures, which are now appearing on some very classy wines, especially in Australia and New Zealand, South Africa and South America.

Decanting

Transferring wine to a decanter brings it into contact with oxygen, which can open up the flavours. You don't need to do this ages before serving and you don't need a special decanter: a glass jug is just as good. And there's no reason why you shouldn't decant the wine to aerate it, then pour it back into its bottle to serve it.

Mature red wine is likely to contain sediment and needs careful handling. Stand the bottle upright for a day or two to let the sediment fall to the bottom. Open the wine carefully, and place a torch or candle beside the decanter. As you pour, stand so that you can see the light shining through the neck of the bottle. Pour the wine into the decanter in one steady motion and stop when you see the sediment reaching the neck of the bottle.

Temperature

The temperature of wine has a bearing on its flavour. Heavy reds are happy at room temperature, but the lighter the wine the cooler it should be. I'd serve Burgundy and other Pinot Noir reds at cool larder temperature. Juicy, fruity young reds, such as wines from the Loire Valley, are refreshing served lightly chilled.

Chilling white wines makes them taste fresher, but also subdues flavours, so bear this in mind if you're splashing out on a top-quality white – don't keep it in the fridge too long. Sparkling wines, however, must be well chilled to avoid exploding corks and fountains of foam.

For quick chilling, fill a bucket with ice and cold water, plus a few spoonfuls of salt if you're in a real hurry. This is much more effective than ice on its own. If the wine is already cool, a vacuum-walled cooler will maintain the temperature.

The wine glass

The ideal wine glass is a fairly large tulip shape, made of fine, clear glass, with a slender stem. This shape helps to concentrate the aromas of the wine and to show off its colours and texture. For sparkling wine choose a tall, slender glass, as it helps the bubbles to last longer.

Look after your glasses carefully. Detergent residues or grease can affect the flavour of any wine and reduce the bubbliness of sparkling wine. Ideally, wash glasses in very hot water and don't use detergent at all. Rinse glasses thoroughly and allow them to air-dry. Store wine glasses upright to avoid trapping stale odours.

Keeping opened bottles

Exposure to oxygen causes wine to deteriorate. Once opened, it will last fairly well for a couple of days if you just push the cork back in and stick the bottle in the fridge, but you can also buy a range of effective devices to help keep oxygen at bay. Vacuvin uses a rubber stopper and a vacuum pump to remove air from the bottle. Others inject inert gas into the bottle to shield the wine from the ravages of oxidation.

Laying down wine

The longer you intend to keep wine before you drink it, the more important it is to store it with care. If you haven't got a cellar, find a nook – under the stairs, a built-in cupboard or a disused fireplace – that is cool, relatively dark and vibration-free, in which you can store the bottles on their sides to keep the corks moist (if a cork dries out it will let air in and spoil the wine).

Wine should be kept cool – around 10–15°C/50–55°F. It is also important to avoid sudden temperature changes or extremes: a windowless garage or outhouse may be cool in summer but may freeze in winter. Exposure to light can ruin wine, but dark bottles go some way to protecting it from light.

How to taste wine

If you just knock your wine back like a cold beer, you'll be missing most of whatever flavour it has to offer. Take a bit of time to pay attention to what you're tasting and I guarantee you'll enjoy the wine more.

Read the label
There's no law that says you have to make life hard for yourself when tasting wine. So have a look at what you're drinking and read the notes on the back label if there is one. The label will tell you the vintage, the region and/or the grape variety, the producer and the alcohol level.

Look at the wine
Pour the wine into a glass so it is a third full and tilt it against a white background so you can enjoy the range of colours in the wine. Is it dark or light? Is it viscous or watery? As you gain experience, the look of the wine will tell you one or two things about the age and the likely flavour and weight of the wine. As a wine ages, whites lose their springtime greenness and gather deeper, golden hues, whereas red wines trade the purple of youth for a paler brick red.

Swirl and sniff
Give the glass a vigorous swirl to wake up the aromas in the wine, stick your nose in and inhale gently. This is where you'll be hit by the amazing range of smells a wine can produce. Interpret them in any way that means something to you personally: it's only by reacting honestly to the taste and smell of a wine that you can build up a memory bank of flavours against which to judge future wines.

Take a sip

At last! It's time to drink the wine. So take a decent-sized slurp – enough to fill your mouth about a third full. The tongue can detect only very basic flavour elements: sweetness at the tip, acidity at the sides and bitterness at the back. The real business of tasting goes on in a cavity at the back of the mouth that is really part of the nose. The idea is to get the fumes from the wine to rise up into this nasal cavity. Note the toughness, acidity and sweetness of the wine, then suck some air through the wine to help the flavours on their way. Gently 'chew' the wine and let it coat your tongue, teeth, cheeks and gums. Jot down a few notes as you form your opinion and then make the final decision… Do you like it or don't you?

Swallow or spit it out

If you are tasting a lot of wines, you will have to spit as you go if you want to remain upright and retain your judgement. Otherwise, go ahead and swallow and enjoy the lovely aftertaste of the wine.

Wine Faults

If you order wine in a restaurant and you find one of these faults you are entitled to a replacement. Many retailers will also replace a faulty bottle if you return it the day after you open it, with your receipt. Sometimes faults affect random bottles, others may ruin a whole case of wine.

• Cork taint – a horrible musty, mouldy smell indicates 'corked' wine, caused by a contaminated cork.

• Volatile acidity – pronounced vinegary or acetone smells.

• Oxidation – sherry-like smells are not appropriate in red and white wines.

• Hydrogen sulphide – 'rotten eggs' smell.

Watchpoints

• Sediment in red wines makes for a gritty, woody mouthful. To avoid this, either decant the wine or simply pour it gently, leaving the last few centilitres of wine in the bottle.

• White crystals, or tartrates, on the cork or at the bottom of bottles of white wine are both harmless and flavourless.

• Sticky bottle neck – if wine has seeped past the cork it probably hasn't been very well kept and air might have got in. This may mean oxidized wine.

• Excess sulphur dioxide is sometimes noticeable as a smell of a recently struck match; it should dissipate after a few minutes.

Wine style guide

When faced with a shelf – or a screen – packed with wines from around the world, where do you start? Well, if you're after a particular flavour, my guide to wine styles will point you in the right direction.

White wines

Bone-dry, neutral whites

Neutral wines exist for the sake of seafood or to avoid interrupting you while you're eating. It's a question of balance, rather than aromas and flavours, but there will be a bit of lemon, yeast and a mineral thrill in a good Muscadet *sur lie* or a proper Chablis. Loads of Italian whites do the same thing, but Italy is increasingly picking up on the global shift towards fruit flavours and maybe some oak. Basic, cheap South African whites are often a good bet if you want something thirst-quenching and easy to drink. Colombard and Chenin are fairly neutral grape varieties widely used in South Africa, often producing appley flavours, and better examples add a lick of honey.

- Muscadet
- Chenin Blanc and Colombard – from the Loire Valley, South-West France, Australia, California or South Africa
- Basic white Bordeaux and Entre-Deux-Mers
- Chablis
- Pinot Grigio

Green, tangy whites

For nerve-tingling refreshment, Sauvignon Blanc is the classic grape, full of fresh grass, gooseberry and nettle flavours. I always used to go for New Zealand versions, but I'm now more inclined to reach for an inexpensive bottle from Chile, South Africa or Hungary. Or even a simple white Bordeaux, because suddenly

Bordeaux Sauvignon is buzzing with life. Most Sancerre and the other Loire Sauvignons are overpriced. Austria's Grüner Veltliner has a peppery freshness. From north-west Iberia, Galicia's Albariño grape has a stony, mineral lemon zest sharpness; the same grape is used in Portugal, for Vinho Verde. Alternatively, look at Riesling: Australia serves it up with aggressive lime and mineral flavours, and New Zealand and Chile give milder versions of the same style. Alsace Riesling is lemony and dry, while German Rieslings go from bone-dry to intensely sweet, with the tangiest, zestiest, coming from the Mosel Valley.

- Sauvignon Blanc – from New Zealand, Chile, Hungary, South Africa, or Bordeaux
- Loire Valley Sauvignons such as Sancerre and Pouilly-Fumé
- Riesling – from Australia, Austria, Chile, Germany, New Zealand, or Alsace in France
- Austrian Grüner Veltliner
- Vinho Verde from Portugal and Albariño from north-west Spain

Intense, nutty whites

The best white Burgundy from the Côte d'Or cannot be bettered for its combination of soft nut and oatmeal flavours, subtle, buttery oak and firm, dry structure. Prices are often hair-raising and the cheaper wines rarely offer much Burgundy style. For around £8 your best bet is oaked Chardonnay from an innovative Spanish region such as Somontano or Navarra. You'll get a nutty, creamy taste and nectarine fruit with good oak-aged white Bordeaux or traditional white Rioja. Top Chardonnays from New World countries – and Italy for that matter – can emulate Burgundy, but once again we're looking at serious prices.

- White Burgundy – including Meursault, Pouilly-Fuissé, Chassagne-Montrachet, Puligny-Montrachet
- White Bordeaux – including Pessac-Léognan, Graves
- White Rioja
- Chardonnay from New Zealand and Oregon – and top examples from Australia, California and South Africa

Ripe, tropical whites

Aussie Chardonnay conquered the world with its upfront flavours of peaches, apricots and melons, usually spiced up by the vanilla, toast and butterscotch richness of new oak. This winning style has now become a standard-issue flavour produced by all sorts of countries, though I still love the original. You'll need to spend a bit more than a fiver nowadays if you want something to relish beyond the first glass. Oaked Australian Semillon can also give rich, ripe fruit flavours, as can oaked Chenin Blanc from New Zealand and South Africa. If you see the words 'unoaked' or 'cool-climate' on an Aussie bottle, expect an altogether leaner drink.

- Chardonnay: from Australia, Chile, California
- Oak-aged Chenin Blanc from New Zealand and South Africa
- Australian Semillon

Aromatic whites

Alsace has always been a plentiful source of perfumed, dry or off-dry whites: Gewurztraminer with its rose and lychee scent or Muscat with its floral, hothouse grape perfume. A few producers in New Zealand, Australia, Chile and South Africa are having some success with these grapes. Floral, apricotty Viognier, traditionally the grape of Condrieu in the northern Rhône, now appears in vins de pays from all over southern France and also from California and Australia. Condrieu is expensive (£20 will get you entry-level stuff and no guarantee that it will be fragrant); vin de pays wines start at around £5 and are just as patchy. For aroma on a budget grab some Hungarian Irsai Olivér or Argentinian Torrontés. English white wines often have a fresh, floral hedgerow scent – the Bacchus grape is one of the leaders of this style.

- Alsace whites, especially Gewurztraminer and Muscat
- Gewürztraminer from Austria, Chile, Germany, New Zealand and cooler regions of Australia
- Condrieu, from the Rhône Valley in France
- Viognier from southern France, Argentina, Australia, California, Chile
- English white wines
- Irsai Olivér from Hungary
- Torrontés from Argentina

Golden, sweet whites

Good sweet wines are difficult to make and therefore expensive: prices for Sauternes and Barsac (from Bordeaux) can go through the roof, but near-neighbours Monbazillac, Loupiac, Saussignac and Ste-Croix-du-Mont are more affordable. Sweet Loire wines such as Quarts de Chaume, Bonnezeaux and some Vouvrays have a quince aroma and a fresh acidity that can keep them lively for decades, as do sweet Rieslings, such as Alsace Vendange Tardive, German and Austrian Beerenauslese (BA), Trockenbeeren-auslese (TBA) and Eiswein. Canadian icewine is quite rare over here, but we're seeing more of Hungary's Tokaji, with its sweet-sour, marmalade flavours.

- Sauternes, Barsac, Loupiac, Sainte-Croix-du-Mont
- Monbazillac, Saussignac
- Loire sweet whites such as Bonnezeaux, Quarts de Chaume and Vouvray moelleux
- Auslese, Beerenauslese and Trockenbeerenauslese from Germany and Austria
- Eiswein from Germany, icewine from Canada
- Botrytis Semillon, Riesling or Gewürztraminer from Australia

Red wines
Juicy, fruity reds

The definitive modern style for easy-going reds. Tasty, refreshing and delicious with or without food, they pack in loads of crunchy fruit while minimizing the tough, gum-drying tannins that characterize most traditional red wine styles. Beaujolais (made from the Gamay grape) is the prototype: the juicy 2006 was very drinkable, and 2007 was pretty good too – you're likely to find both vintages in the shops now. And if you're distinctly underwhelmed by the very mention of the word 'Beaujolais', remember that the delightfully named Fleurie, St-Amour and Chiroubles also come from the Beaujolais region. Loire reds such as Chinon and Saumur (made from Cabernet Franc) pack in the fresh raspberries. Italy's Bardolino is light and refreshing, as is young Valpolicella. Nowadays, hi-tech producers all over the world are working the magic with a whole host of grape varieties. Carmenère, Malbec and Merlot are always good bets, and Grenache/Garnacha and Tempranillo usually come up with the goods. Italian grapes like Bonarda, Barbera and Sangiovese seem to double in succulence under Argentina's blazing sun. And at around £6 even Cabernet Sauvignon – if it's from somewhere warm like Australia, South America, South Africa or Spain – or a vin de pays Syrah from southern France, will emphasize the fruit and hold back on the tannin.

- Beaujolais – including Brouilly, Chiroubles, Fleurie, Juliénas, Moulin-à-Vent, St-Amour. Also wines made from the Gamay grape in other parts of France
- Loire reds: Chinon, Saumur, Saumur-Champigny – and, if you're lucky, Bourgueil, Cheverny and St-Nicolas de Bourgueil
- Grenache (from France) and Garnacha (from Spain)
- Carmenère from Chile and basic Merlot from just about anywhere
- Inexpensive Argentinian reds, especially Bonarda, but also Sangiovese and Tempranillo

Silky, strawberryish reds

Here we're looking for some special qualities, specifically a gorgeously smooth texture and a heavenly fragrance of strawberries, raspberries or cherries. We're looking for soft, decadent, seductive wines. One grape – Pinot Noir – and one region – Burgundy – stand out, but prices are high to astronomical. Good red Burgundy is addictively hedonistic and all sorts of strange decaying aromas start to hover around the strawberries as the wine ages. Pinot Noirs from New Zealand, California, Oregon and, increasingly, Australia come close, but they're expensive, too; Chilean Pinots are far more affordable. You can get that strawberry perfume (though not the silky texture) from other grapes in Spain's Navarra, Rioja and up-coming regions like La Mancha and Murcia. Southern Rhône blends can deliver if you look for fairly light examples of Côtes du Rhône-Villages or Costières de Nîmes.

- Red Burgundy – including Chassagne-Montrachet, Beaune, Givry, Nuits-St-Georges, Pommard
- Pinot Noir from Australia, California, Chile, New Zealand, Oregon
- Spanish reds from Rioja, Navarra, La Mancha and Valdepeñas, especially with Tempranillo as the main grape
- Red blends from the southern Rhône Valley, such as Costières de Nîmes, Côtes du Rhône-Villages, Gigondas
- Australian Grenache

Intense, blackcurranty reds

Firm, intense wines which often only reveal their softer side with a bit of age; Cabernet Sauvignon is the grape, on its own or blended with Merlot or other varieties. Bordeaux is the classic region but there are far too many overpriced underachievers there. And Cabernet's image has changed. You can still choose the austere, tannic style, in theory aging to a heavenly cassis and cedar maturity, but most of the world is taking a fruitier blackcurrant-and-mint approach. Chile does the fruity style par excellence. New Zealand can deliver Bordeaux-like flavours, but in a faster-maturing wine. Australia often adds a medicinal eucalyptus twist or a dollop of blackcurrant jam. Argentina and South Africa are making their mark too.

- Bordeaux reds such as Côtes de Castillon, St-Émilion, Pomerol
- Cabernet Sauvignon from just about anywhere
- Cabernet Sauvignon-Merlot blends

Spicy, warm-hearted reds

Australian Shiraz is the epitome of this rumbustious, riproaring style: dense, rich, chocolaty, sometimes with a twist of pepper, a whiff of smoke, or a slap of leather. But it's not alone. There are southern Italy's Primitivo and Nero d'Avola, California's Zinfandel, Mexico's Petite Sirah, Argentina's Malbec, South Africa's Pinotage, Toro from Spain and some magnificent Greek reds. In southern France the wines of the Languedoc often show this kind of warmth, roughed up with hillside herbs. And if you want your spice more serious, more smoky and minerally, go for the classic wines of the northern Rhône Valley.

- Australian Shiraz, as well as blends of Shiraz with Grenache and Mourvèdre/Mataro – and Durif
- Northern Rhône Syrah (Cornas, Côte-Rôtie, Hermitage, St-Joseph) and southern Rhône blends such as Châteauneuf-du-Pape
- Southern French reds, such as Corbières, Coteaux du Languedoc, Côtes du Roussillon, Faugères, Fitou, Minervois
- Italian reds such as Primitivo, Aglianico, Negroamaro and Nero d'Avola
- Zinfandel and Petite Sirah reds
- Argentinian Malbec

Mouthwatering, sweet-sour reds

Sounds weird? This style is primarily the preserve of Italy, and it's all about food: the rasp of sourness cuts through rich, meaty food, with a lip-smacking tingle that works equally well with pizza or tomato-based pasta dishes. But there's fruit in there too – cherries and plums – plus raisiny sweetness and a herby bite. The wines are now better made than ever, with more seductive fruit, but holding on to those fascinating flavours. All sorts of native Italian grape varieties deliver this delicious sour-cherries taste: Sangiovese (the classic red grape of Tuscany), Nebbiolo (from Piedmont), Barbera, Dolcetto, Teroldego, Sagrantino… You'll have to shell out up to a tenner for decent Chianti, more for Piedmont wines (especially Barolo and Barbaresco, so try Langhe instead). Valpolicella can be very good, but choose with care. Portugal reveals something of the same character in its reds.

- Chianti, plus other wines made from the Sangiovese grape
- Barolo, Barbaresco and other wines made from the Nebbiolo grape
- Valpolicella Classico, Amarone della Valpolicella
- Southern Italian reds
- Touriga Nacional and other Portuguese reds

Delicate (and not-so-delicate) rosé

Dry rosé can be wonderful, with flavours of strawberries and maybe raspberries and rosehips, cherries, apples and herbs, too. Look for wines made from sturdy grapes like Cabernet, Syrah or Merlot, or go for Grenache/Garnacha or Tempranillo from Spain and the Rhône Valley. South America is a good bet for flavoursome, fruit-forward pink wine. *See pages 102–7 for my top pinks this year.*

Drink organic – or even biodynamic

- The widely discussed benefits of organic farming – respect for the environment, minimal chemical residues in our food and drink – apply to grapes as much as to any other produce. Full-blown organic viticulture forbids the use of synthetic fertilizers, herbicides or fungicides; instead, cover crops and companion planting encourage biodiversity and natural predators to keep the soil and vines healthy. Warm, dry climates like the South of France, Chile and South Africa have the advantage of rarely suffering from the damp that can cause rot, mildew and other problems – we should be seeing more organic wines from these regions. Organic wines from European countries are often labelled 'Biologique', or simply 'Bio'.
- Biodynamic viticulture takes working with nature one stage further: work in the vineyard is planned in accordance with the movements of the planets, moon, sun and cosmic forces to achieve health and balance in the soil and in the vine. Vines are treated with infusions of mineral, animal and plant materials, applied in homeopathic quantities, with some astonishing results.
- If you want to know more, the best companies to contact are Vinceremos and Vintage Roots (see page 187).

Sparkling wines

Champagne can be the finest sparkling wine on the planet, but fizz made by the traditional Champagne method in Australia, New Zealand or California – often using the same grape varieties – is often just as good and cheaper. It might be a little more fruity, where Champagne concentrates on bready, yeasty or nutty aromas, but a few are dead ringers for the classic style. Fizz is also made in other parts of France: Crémant de Bourgogne is one of the best. England is beginning to show its potential. Italy's Prosecco is soft and delicately scented. Spain's Cava is perfect party fizz available at bargain basement prices in all the big supermarkets.

• Champagne
• Traditional method fizz made from Chardonnay, Pinot Noir and Pinot Meunier grapes grown in Australia, California, England, New Zealand, South Africa
• Crémant de Bourgogne, Crémant de Loire, Crémant de Jura, Crémant d'Alsace, Blanquette de Limoux
• Cava
• Prosecco
• Sekt is Germany's sparkling wine, and is occasionally 100 per cent Riesling
• Lambrusco from Italy is gently sparkling and usually red
• Sparkling Shiraz – an Aussie speciality – will make a splash at a wild party

Fortified wines

Tangy, appetizing fortified wines

To set your taste buds tingling, fino and manzanilla sherries are pale, perfumed, bone dry and bracingly tangy. True amontillado, dark and nutty, is also dry. Dry oloroso adds deep, raisiny flavours. Palo cortado falls between amontillado and oloroso; manzanilla pasada is an older, nuttier manzanilla. The driest style of Madeira, Sercial, is steely and smoky; Verdelho Madeira is a bit fuller and richer, but still tangy and dry.

- Manzanilla and fino sherry
- Dry amontillado, palo cortado and dry oloroso sherry
- Sercial and Verdelho Madeira

Rich, warming fortified wines

Raisins and brown sugar, dried figs and caramelized nuts – do you like the sound of that? Port is the classic dark sweet wine, and it comes in several styles, from basic ruby, to tawny, matured in cask for 10 years or more, to vintage, which matures to mellowness in the bottle. The Portuguese island of Madeira produces fortified wines with rich brown smoky flavours and a startling bite of acidity: the sweet styles to look for are Bual and Malmsey. Decent sweet sherries are rare; oloroso dulce is a style with stunningly concentrated flavours. In southern France, Banyuls and Maury are deeply fruity fortified wines. Marsala, from Sicily, has rich brown sugar flavours with a refreshing sliver of acidity. The versatile Muscat grape makes luscious golden wines all around the Mediterranean, but also pops up in orange, black, and the gloriously rich, treacly brown versions that Australia does superbly.

- Port
- Bual and Malmsey Madeira
- Marsala
- Rich, sweet sherry styles include Pedro Ximénez, oloroso dulce
- Vins doux naturels from southern France: Banyuls, Maury
- Fortified (liqueur) Muscat 'stickies' from Australia

Buying wine for the long term

Most of this book is about wines to drink more or less immediately – that's how modern wines are made, and that's what you'll find in most High Street retail outlets. If you're looking for a mature vintage of a great wine that's ready to drink – or are prepared to wait 10 years or more for a great vintage to reach its peak – specialist wine merchants will be able to help; the Internet's another good place to look for mature wines. Here's my beginners' guide to buying wine for drinking over the longer term.

Auctions

A wine sale catalogue from one of the UK's auction houses will have wine enthusiasts drooling over names they certainly don't see every day. Better still, the lots are often of mature vintages that are ready to drink. Before you go, find out all you can about the producer and vintages described in the catalogue. My annually updated *Pocket Wine Book* is a good place to start, or *Michael Broadbent's Vintage Wines* for old and rare wines; the national wine magazines (*Decanter, Wine & Spirit*) run regular features on wine regions and their vintages. You can also learn a lot from tutored tastings – especially 'vertical' tastings, which compare different vintages. This is important – some merchants take the opportunity to clear inferior vintages at auction.

The drawbacks? You have no guarantee that the wine has been well stored, and if it's faulty you have little chance of redress. As prices of the most sought-after wines have soared, so it has become profitable either to forge the bottles and their contents or to try to pass off stock that is clearly out of condition. But for expensive and mature wines, I have to say that the top auction houses make a considerable effort to check the provenance and integrity of the wines. Don't forget that there will usually be a commission, or buyers' premium, to pay, so check out the small print in the sale catalogue. Online wine auctions have similar pros and cons.

If you've never bought wine at an auction before, a good place to start would be a local auctioneer such as Straker Chadwick in Abergavenny (tel: 01873 852624, www.strakerchadwick.co.uk) or Morphets in Harrogate (tel: 01423 530030, www.morphets.co.uk); they're less intimidating than the famous London houses of Christie's and Sotheby's and you may come away with some really exciting wine.

Buying en primeur

En primeur is a French term for wine which is sold before it is bottled, sometimes referred to as a 'future'. In the spring after the vintage, the Bordeaux châteaux – and a few other wine-producing regions – hold tastings of barrel samples for members of the international wine trade. The châteaux then offer a proportion of their production to the wine merchants (*négociants*) in Bordeaux, who in turn offer it to wine merchants around the world at an opening price.

The advantage to the châteaux is that their capital is not tied up in expensive stock for the next year or two, until the wines are bottled and ready to ship. Traditionally merchants would buy en primeur for stock to be sold later at a higher price, while offering their customers the chance to take advantage of the opening prices as well. The idea of private individuals investing rather than institutions took off with a series of good Bordeaux vintages in the 1980s; it's got ever more hectic since then.

Wine for the future

There is a lot to be said for buying en primeur. For one thing, in a great vintage you may be able to find the finest and rarest wines far more cheaply than they will ever appear again. Every classic vintage in Bordeaux opens at a higher and higher price, but that price never drops, and so the top wines increase in value, whatever price they start at. Equally, when a wine – even a relatively inexpensive one – is made in very limited quantities, buying en primeur may be practically your only chance of getting hold of it.

In the past, British wine merchants and their privileged customers were able to 'buy double what you want, sell half for double what you paid, and drink for free', but as the market has opened up to people more interested in making a quick buck than drinking fine wine, the whole process has become more risky.

Another potential hazard is that a tasting assessment is difficult at an early date. There is a well-founded suspicion that many barrel samples are doctored (legally) to appeal to the most powerful consumer critics, in particular the American Robert Parker and the *Wine Spectator* magazine. The wine that is finally bottled may or may not bear a resemblance to what was tasted in the spring following the vintage. In any case, most serious red wines are in a difficult stage of their evolution in the spring, and with the best will in the world it is possible to get one's evaluation wrong. However, the aforementioned Americans, and magazines like *Decanter* and *Wine & Spirit*, will do their best to offer you accurate judgements on the newly offered wines, and most merchants who make a primeur offer also write a good assessment of the wines. You will find that many of them quote the Parker or *Wine Spectator* marks. Anything over 90 out of 100 risks being hyped and hiked in price. Many of the best bargains get marks between 85 and 89, since the 90+ marks are generally awarded for power rather than subtlety. Consideration can be given to the producer's reputation for consistency and to the general vintage assessment for the region.

Prices can go down as well as up. They may not increase significantly for some years after the campaign.

Some popular vintages are offered at ridiculously high prices – some unpopular ones too. It's only about twice a decade that the combination of high quality and fair prices offers the private buyer a chance of a good, guaranteed profit. Interestingly, if one highly-touted vintage is followed by another, the prices for the second one often have to fall because the market simply will not accept two inflated price structures in a row. Recent Bordeaux examples of this are the excellent 1990 after the much hyped 1989 and the potentially fine 2001 after the understandably hyped 2000.

Bordeaux vintage update

2004 was a bigger, more classic, but more erratic vintage than 2003 in Bordeaux; the good news is that prices dropped by a third. A lot of people didn't buy the 2004 – and it was overshadowed by the 2005 – but don't overlook it: there's some absolutely smashing stuff at very reasonable prices. The superlative 2005 vintage is certainly one of the best ever – but prices are some of the highest ever and continue to climb. Both of these vintages have now been bottled, and you should be able to find a good Fourth or Fifth Growth for £20–30 a bottle – a First Growth will set you back £800–1000. 2006 is a much more patchy vintage, though some very tasty stuff was made. Opening prices were not much cheaper than 2005, but they haven't moved much.

2007 is generally a lighter vintage than 2005 and 06 – remember the soggy summer? The sun came out again in September, though, so it wasn't a complete washout. Even so, there won't be any bargains: the burgeoning market for fine wine is being led by Russia, China and India and buyers there will already have snapped up the top labels. Wines at lower levels won't rise in price over the next two or three years, so this is not a vintage for investors.

Secure cellarage

Another worry is that the merchant you buy the wine from may not still be around to deliver it to you two years later. Buy from a well-established merchant you trust, with a solid trading base in other wines.

Once the wines are shipped you may want your merchant to store the wine for you; there is usually a small charge for this. If your merchant offers cellarage, you should insist that (1) you receive a stock certificate; (2) your wines are stored separately from the merchant's own stocks; and (3) your cases are identifiable as your property. All good merchants offer these safeguards as a minimum service.

Check the small print

Traditional wine merchants may quote prices exclusive of VAT and/or duty: wine may not be the bargain it first appears. A wine quoted en primeur is usually offered on an ex-cellars (EC) basis; the price excludes shipping, duties and taxes such as VAT. A price quoted in bond (IB) in the UK includes shipping, but excludes duties and taxes. Duty paid (DP) prices exclude VAT. You should check beforehand the exact terms of sale with your merchant, who will give you a projection of the final 'duty paid delivered' price.

Retailers' directory

All these retailers have been chosen on the basis of the quality and interest of their lists. If you want to find a local retailer, turn to the Who's Where directory on page 192. Case = 12 bottles

The following services are available where indicated:
C = cellarage   **G** = glass hire/loan   **M** = mail/online order   **T** = tastings and talks

A & B Vintners

Little Tawsden, Spout Lane, Brenchley, Kent TN12 7AS (01892) 724977
fax (01892) 722673 e-mail info@abvintners.co.uk website www.abvintners.co.uk
hours Mon–Fri 9–6 cards MasterCard, Visa delivery Free 5 cases or more, otherwise £11.75 per consignment UK mainland minimum order 1 mixed case en primeur Burgundy, Languedoc, Rhône. C M T
✪ *Specialists in Burgundy, the Rhône and southern France, with a string of top-quality domaines from all three regions.*

Adnams

head office & mail order Sole Bay Brewery, Southwold, Suffolk IP18 6JW (01502) 727222
fax (01502) 727223 e-mail wines@adnams.co.uk website www.adnams.co.uk
shops • Adnams Wine Shop, Pinkney's Lane, Southwold, Suffolk IP18 6EW • Adnams Cellar & Kitchen Stores: Victoria Street, Southwold, Suffolk IP18 6JW • The Old School House, Park Road, Holkham, Wells-next-the-Sea, Norfolk NR23 1AB (01328) 711714 • Station Road, Woodbridge, Suffolk IP12 4AU (01394) 386594 • Bath Row Warehouse, St Mary's Passage, Stamford, Lincolnshire PE9 2HG (01780) 753127 • The Cardinal's Hat, 23 The Thoroughfare, Harleston, Norfolk IP20 9AS (01379) 854788 • 1 Market Street, Saffron Walden, Essex CB10 1JB (01799) 527281 • 23a Lees Yard, Off Bull Street, Holt, Norfolk NR25 6HS (01263) 715558 • 73–75 High Street, Hadleigh, Suffolk IP7 5DY (01473) 827796 • 26 Hill Rise, Richmond-upon-Thames, Surrey TW10 6UA (020) 8940 8684
hours (Orderline) Mon–Fri 9–6.00; Cellar & Kitchen Store Southwold: Mon–Sat 9–6, Sun 11–4; Wine Shop Southwold: Mon–Sat 9.30–5.30, Sun 11–4; Holkham, Woodbridge and Stamford: Mon–Sat 10–6, Sun 11–4; Harleston: Mon–Sat 10–6; Holt: Mon–Sat 8.30–6, Sun 11–4; Hadleigh: Mon–Sat 9–6, Sun 11–4; Saffron Walden and Richmond: Mon–Sat 9–7, Sun 11–4 cards Maestro, MasterCard, Visa, Delta discounts 5% for 3 cases or more, 10% for 5 cases or more

delivery Free for orders over £125 in most of mainland UK, otherwise £7.50 en primeur Bordeaux, Burgundy, Chile, Rhône.
✪ *Extensive list of personality-packed wines from around the world, chosen by Adnams' enthusiastic team of buyers.*

Aldi Stores

PO Box 26, Atherstone, Warwickshire CV9 2SH; 345 stores store location line 08705 134262
website www.aldi-stores.co.uk hours Mon–Wed 9–6, Thurs–Fri 9–7, Sat 8.30–5.30, Sun 10–4 (selected stores); check
the website for opening times of nearest store cards Maestro, Visa (debit only).
✪ *Decent everyday stuff from around the world, with lots of wines under £4.*

armit

5 Royalty Studios, 105 Lancaster Road, London W11 1QF (020) 7908 0600
fax (020) 7908 0601 e-mail info@armit.co.uk website www.armit.co.uk hours Mon–Fri 9–5.30
cards Maestro, MasterCard, Visa delivery Free for orders over £250, otherwise £15 delivery charge
minimum order 1 case en primeur Bordeaux, Burgundy, Italy, Rhône, New World. C M T
✪ *Particularly strong on wines to go with food – they supply some of the country's top restaurants.*

ASDA

head office Asda House, Southbank, Great Wilson Street, Leeds LS11 5AD (0113) 243 5435
fax (0113) 241 8666 customer service (0500) 100055; 329 stores website www.asda.co.uk
hours Selected stores open 24 hrs, see local store for details cards Maestro, MasterCard, Visa.
✪ *Great value – lots under a fiver – and a large range of interesting wines, especially in the Extra Special range.*

Australian Wine Centre

mail order only PO Box 3854, Datchet, Slough SL3 3EN fax 01753 591369
email customerservice@australianwinecentre.co.uk website www.australianwinecentre.co.uk cards MasterCard, Visa
delivery Free for orders over £100, otherwise £5 per order; UK mainland only minimum order 1 mixed case.
✪ *Some brilliant Australian wines.*

Averys Wine Merchants

4 High Street, Nailsea, Bristol BS48 1BT 0845 863 0995
fax (01275) 811101 e-mail sales@averys.com website www.averys.com

• Shop and Cellars, 9 Culver Street, Bristol BS1 5LD (0117) 921 4146 fax (0117) 922 6318
e-mail cellars@averys.com hours Mon–Fri 9–7, Sat 9.30–5.30, Sun 10–4; Shop Mon–Sat 9–7
cards Maestro, MasterCard, Visa discounts Monthly mail order offers, Discover Wine with Averys 13th bottle free
delivery £5.99 per delivery address en primeur Bordeaux, Burgundy, Port, Rhône. C G M T
✪ *A small but very respectable selection from just about everywhere in France, Italy, Spain and Germany, as well as some good New World wines.*

Bacchus Wine

38 Market Place, Olney, Bucks MK46 4AJ (01234) 711140
e-mail wine@bacchus.co.uk website www.bacchus.co.uk hours Tue–Fri 10.30–7, Sat 9.30–6, Sun 12–4 cards AmEx, Maestro, MasterCard, Visa delivery £5 per dozen, local only minimum order 1 case. G M T
✪ *France and Italy have the broadest coverage and you'll find many wines under £10.*

Ballantynes Wine Merchants

211–217 Cathedral Road, Cardiff CF11 9PP (02920) 222202
fax (02920) 222112 e-mail rlchard@ballantynes.co.uk website www.ballantynes.co.uk
hours Mon–Fri 9.30–6.30, Sat 9.30–5.30 cards Access, Maestro, MasterCard, Visa discounts 8% on collection of more than 12 bottles delivery Free for orders over £90; £9.99 for first case; £4.99 for subsequent cases minimum order £50 (mail order) en primeur Bordeaux, Burgundy, Italy, Rhône. C G M T
✪ *Italy, Burgundy, Rhône and Languedoc-Roussillon are stunning, most regions of France are well represented and there's some terrific stuff from Australia, New Zealand and Spain.*

Balls Brothers

313 Cambridge Heath Road, London E2 9LQ (020) 7739 1642
fax 0870 243 9775 direct sales (020) 7739 1642 e-mail wine@ballsbrothers.co.uk
website www.ballsbrothers.co.uk hours Mon–Fri 9–5.30 cards AmEx, Diners, Maestro, MasterCard, Visa
delivery Free 1 case or more locally; £9 for 1 case, free for 2 cases or more, England, Wales and Scottish Lowlands; islands and Scottish Highlands phone for details. G M T
✪ *French specialist – you'll find something of interest from most regions – with older vintages available. Spain and Australia are also very good. Many of the wines can be enjoyed in Balls Brothers' London wine bars and restaurants.*

The following services are available where indicated: **C** = cellarage **G** = glass hire/loan **M** = mail/online order **T** = tastings and talks

H & H Bancroft Wines

1 China Wharf, 29 Mill Street, London SE1 2BQ (020) 7232 5450

fax (020) 7232 5451 e-mail sales@bancroftwines.com website www.bancroftwines.com hours Mon–Fri 9–5.30
cards Delta, Maestro, MasterCard, Visa discounts Negotiable delivery £15 for 1–2 cases in mainland UK; free 3 cases
or more or for an order value of £300 or more. minimum order 1 case en primeur Bordeaux, Burgundy, Rhône. C M T
✪ *Bancroft are UK agents for an impressive flotilla of French winemakers: Burgundy, Rhône, Loire and some interesting
wines from southern France. There is plenty of New World, too, and even wines from Slovenia.*

Bat & Bottle

office The Treehouse, 9 Ashwell Road, Oakham LE15 6QG (01572) 759735
warehouse Unit 5, 19 Pillings Road, Oakham LE15 6QF fax 0870 458 2505 e-mail post@batwine.co.uk
website www.batwine.co.uk hours Warehouse: Sat 9–2, other times by arrangement cards Maestro, MasterCard, Visa
delivery Free for orders over £150. G M T
✪ *Ben and Emma Robson specialize in Italy, and in characterful wines from small producers.*

Bennetts Fine Wines

High Street, Chipping Campden, Glos GL55 6AG (01386) 840392 fax (01386) 840974
e-mail enquiries@bennettsfinewines.com website www.bennettsfinewines.com hours Tues–Sat 9.30–6
cards Access, Maestro, MasterCard, Visa discounts On collected orders of 1 case or more delivery £6 per case,
minimum charge £12, free for orders over £200 en primeur Burgundy, California, Rhône, New Zealand. G M T
✪ *Reasonable prices for high-calibre producers – there's lots to choose from at around £10. Mainly from France and Italy,
but some good German, Spanish and Portuguese wines, too.*

Berkmann Wine Cellars

10–12 Brewery Road, London N7 9NH (020) 7609 4711 fax (020) 7607 0018 e-mail orders@berkmann.co.uk
• Brunel Park, Vincients Road, Bumpers Farm, Chippenham, Wiltshire SN14 6NQ (01249) 463501
fax (01249) 463502 e-mail orders.chippenham@berkmann.co.uk
• Brian Coad Wine Cellars, 41b Valley Road, Plympton, Plymouth, Devon PL7 1RF (01752) 334970 fax (01752) 346540
e-mail orders.briancoad@berkmann.co.uk
• Pagendam Pratt Wine Cellars, 16 Marston Moor Business Park, Rudgate, Tockwith, North Yorkshire YO26 7QF
(01423) 357567 fax (01423) 357568 e-mail orders@pagendampratt.co.uk
• T M Robertson Wine Cellars, Unit 12, A1 Industrial Estate, 232 Sir Harry Lauder Road, Portobello, Edinburgh EH15 2QA

(0131) 657 6390 fax (0131) 657 6389 e-mail orders@tmrobertson.co.uk

• Churchill Vintners, 401 Walsall Road, Perry Bar, Birmingham B42 1BT (0121) 356 8888

fax (0121) 356 1111 e-mail info@churchill-vintners.co.uk

website www.berkmann.co.uk hours Mon–Fri 9–5.30 cards Maestro, MasterCard, Visa

discounts £3 per unmixed case collected delivery Free for orders over £120 to UK mainland (excluding the Highlands)

minimum order 1 mixed case. C G M

✪ *UK agent for, among others, Antinori, Casa Lapostolle, Chapel Hill, Chivite, Deutz, Duboeuf, Mastroberardino, Masi, Norton, Rioja Alta and Tasca d'Almerita. An incredibly diverse list, with some great Italian wines.*

Berry Bros. & Rudd

3 St James's Street, London SW1A 1EG 0870 900 4300

sales and services 0870 900 4300 (lines open Mon–Fri 9–6) fax 0870 900 4301

• Berrys' Factory Outlet, Hamilton Close, Houndmills, Basingstoke, Hampshire RG21 6YB 0870 900 4300

e-mail bbr@bbr.com website www.bbr.com hours St James's Street: Mon–Fri 10–6, Sat 10–5; Berrys' Factory Outlet: Mon–Fri 10–6, Sat–Sun 10–4 cards AmEx, Diners, Maestro, MasterCard, Visa discounts Variable

delivery Free for orders of £200 or more, otherwise £10 en primeur Bordeaux, Burgundy, Rhône. C G M T

✪ *Classy and wide-ranging list. There's an emphasis on the classic regions of France. Berry's Own Selection is extensive, with wines made by world-class producers.*

Bibendum Wine Limited

mail order 113 Regents Park Road, London NW1 8UR (020) 7449 4120

fax (020) 7449 4121 e-mail sales@bibendum-wine.co.uk website www.bibendum-wine.co.uk

hours Mon–Fri 9–6 cards Maestro, MasterCard, Visa delivery Free throughout mainland UK for orders over £250,

otherwise £15 en primeur Bordeaux, Burgundy, New World, Rhône, Port. M T

✪ *Equally strong in the Old World and the New: Huet in Vouvray and Lageder in Alto Adige are matched by d'Arenberg and Katnook from Australia and Catena Zapata from Argentina.*

Big Red Wine Company

mail order Barton Coach House, The Street, Barton Mills, Suffolk IP28 6AA (01638) 510803

e-mail sales@bigredwine.co.uk website www.bigredwine.co.uk hours Mon–Sat 9–6

cards AmEx, Delta, Maestro, Mastercard, Visa, PayPal discounts 5–15% for Wine Club members and on occasional offers;

minimum £3 unmixed case discount; discounts for large orders negotiable delivery £5 per consignment for orders under

£150, £10 for orders under £50, UK mainland en primeur Bordeaux, Rhône. C G M T

✪ *Intelligently chosen, reliably individualistic wines from good estates in France, Italy and Spain. A list worth reading, full of information and provocative opinion – and they're not overcharging.*

Booths

Booths, Booths Central Office, Longridge Road, Ribbleton, Preston PR2 5BX (01772) 693800
fax (01772) 693893; 26 stores across the North of England website www.booths.co.uk and www.booths-wine.co.uk
hours Office: Mon–Fri 8.30–5; shop hours vary cards AmEx, Electron, Maestro, MasterCard, Solo, Visa
discounts 5% off any 6 bottles. G T

✪ *A list for any merchant to be proud of, never mind a supermarket. There's plenty around £5, but if you're prepared to hand over £7–9 you'll find some really interesting stuff.*

Bordeaux Index

10 Hatton Garden, London EC1N 8AH (020) 7207 0700
fax (020) 7490 1955 e-mail sales@bordeauxindex.com website www.bordeauxindex.com hours Mon–Fri 8.30–6
cards AmEx, Maestro, MasterCard, Visa, JCB (transaction fees apply) delivery (Private sales only) free for orders over
£2000 UK mainland; others at cost minimum order £500 en primeur Bordeaux, Burgundy, Rhône, Italy. C T

✪ *An extensive list for big spenders, with pages and pages of Bordeaux, including Yquem, white Burgundy and vintage Champagne. You'll also find interesting stuff from Italy, Australia and America.*

Budgens Stores

head office Musgrave House, Widewater Place, Moorhall Road, Harefield, Uxbridge, Middlesex UB9 6NS 0870 050 0158
fax 0870 400 6094, 190 stores mainly in southern England and East Anglia – for nearest store call 0800 526002
e-mail info@ budgens.co.uk website www.budgens.co.uk hours Variable according to size and location; usually
Mon–Sat 8–8, Sun 10–4 cards Maestro, MasterCard, Solo, Visa.

✪ *These days you can be reasonably confident of going into Budgens and coming out with something you'd really like to drink.*

The Butlers Wine Cellar

247 Queens Park Road, Brighton BN2 9XJ (01273) 698724
fax (01273) 622761 e-mail henry@butlers-winecellar.co.uk website www.butlers-winecellar.co.uk
hours Tue–Sat 11–7 cards Access, AmEx, Maestro, MasterCard, Visa delivery Free locally 1 case or more; free UK
mainland 3 cases or more en primeur Bordeaux. G M T

✪ *Henry Butler personally chooses all the wines on the regular list and there is some fascinating stuff there, including English wines from local growers such as Breaky Bottom and Ridgeview. The rosés include English fizz and a delicious wine from Bonny Doon in California. Check the website or join the mailing list as offers change regularly.*

Anthony Byrne

mail order Ramsey Business Park, Stocking Fen Road, Ramsey, Cambs PE26 2UR (01487) 814555
fax (01487) 814962 e-mail anthony@abfw.co.uk or gary@abfw.co.uk website www.abfw.co.uk
hours Mon–Fri 9–5.30 cards MasterCard, Visa discounts Available on cases delivery Free 5 cases or more, or orders of £250 or more; otherwise £12 minimum order 1 case en primeur Bordeaux, Burgundy, Rhône. C M T
✪ *A serious range of Burgundy; smaller but focused lists from Bordeaux and the Rhône; carefully selected wines from Alsace, Loire and Provence; and a wide range of New World.*

D Byrne & Co

Victoria Buildings, 12 King Street, Clitheroe, Lancashire BB7 2EP (01200) 423152
hours Mon–Sat 8.30–6 cards Maestro, MasterCard, Visa delivery Free within 50 miles; nationally £20 1st case, £5 subsequent cases en primeur Bordeaux, Burgundy, Rhône, Germany. G M T
✪ *One of northern England's best wine merchants, with a hugely impressive range. I urge you to go see for yourself.*

Cambridge Wine Merchants

head office 29 Dry Drayton Industries, Scotland Road, Dry Drayton, CB23 8AT (01954) 214528
fax (01954) 214574 e-mail info @cambridgewine.com website www.cambridgewine.com
• 42 Mill Road, Cambridge CB1 2AD (01223) 568993 e-mail mill@cambridgewine.com
• 32 Bridge Street, Cambridge CB2 1UJ (01223) 568989 e-mail bridge@cambridgewine.com
• 2 King's Parade, Cambridge CB2 1SJ (01223) 309309 e-mail kings@cambridgewine.com
• 34b Kneesworth Street, Royston SG8 5AB (01763) 247076 e-mail royston@cambridgewine.com
• Edinburgh Wine Merchants, 30b Raeburn Place, Edinburgh (0131) 343 2347 e-mail stockbridge@edinburghwine.com
hours Mon–Sat 10am– 9pm, Sun 12-8pm cards Amex, MasterCard, Switch, Visa discounts Buy 4, get the cheapest one free (selected lines) delivery Free for 12 bottles or more within 5 miles of Cambridge; £2.50 for under 12 bottles. National delivery £5.99 per case of 12 bottles; £9.99 for 1 to 11 bottles. en primeur Bordeaux, Burgundy, Rhône, Port. C G M T
✪ *Young, unstuffy merchants with a well-chosen list: no dross, just a tight focus on good, individual producers, with particularly interesting German, Champagne and dessert sections. They're also very serious about port – as befits their university roots. Informative monthly newsletter. Every branch has a wine tasting club.*

Cape Wine and Food

77 Laleham Road, Staines, Middlesex TW18 2EA (01784) 451860
fax (01784) 469267 e-mail ross@capewineandfood.com website www.capewineandfood.com
hours Mon–Sat 10–6, Sun 10–5 cards Maestro, MasterCard, Visa discounts 10% mixed case. G M T
✪ *If you're looking for South African wine, this shop is the place to visit. Alongside wines for everyday drinking, there are some of the Cape's top red blends, going up to around £50 a bottle.*

Les Caves de Pyrene

Pew Corner, Old Portsmouth Road, Artington, Guildford GU3 1LP (office) (01483) 538820 (shop) (01483) 554750
fax (01483) 455068 e-mail sales@lescaves.co.uk website www.lescaves.co.uk
hours Mon–Fri 9–5 cards Maestro, MasterCard, Visa delivery Free for orders over £180 within M25, elsewhere at cost discounts Negotiable minimum order 1 mixed case en primeur South-West France. G M T
✪ *Excellent operation, devoted to seeking out top wines from all over southern France. Other areas of France are looking increasingly good too, Italy's regions are well represented, and there's some choice stuff from New Zealand.*

ChateauOnline

mail order BP68, 39602 Arbois Cedex, France (0033) 3 84 66 42 21
fax (0033) 1 55 30 31 41 customer service 0800 169 2736 website www.chateauonline.com
hours Mon–Fri 8–11.30, 12.30–4.30 cards AmEx, Maestro, MasterCard, Visa
delivery £7.99 per consignment en primeur Bordeaux, Burgundy, Languedoc-Roussillon.
✪ *French specialist, with an impressive list of over 2000 wines. Easy-to-use website with a well-thought-out range of mixed cases, frequent special offers and bin end sales.*

Chilean Wine Club

1 Cannon Meadow, Bull Lane, Gerrards Cross, Buckinghamshire SL9 8RE (01753) 890319
e-mail info@chileanwineclub.co.uk website www.chileanwineclub.co.uk cards Delta, Maestro, Mastercard, Visa
delivery £5.99 per address; free for orders over £250 in UK mainland; free to postcode SL9 irrespective of number of cases minimum order 1 mixed case.
✪ *A one-stop shop for many of Chile's finest wines that are not available on the High Street. If it happens in Chile, you will hear about it here first.*

The following services are available where indicated: **C** = cellarage **G** = glass hire/loan **M** = mail/online order **T** = tastings and talks

Cockburns of Leith

Cockburn House, Unit 3, Abbeyhill Industrial Estate, Abbey Lane, Edinburgh EH8 8HL (0131) 661 8400
fax (0131) 661 7333 e-mail sales@cockburnsofleith.co.uk
website www.cockburnsofleith.co.uk hours Mon–Fri 9–6; Sat 10–5 cards Maestro, MasterCard, Visa
delivery Free 12 or more bottles within Edinburgh; elsewhere £7 1–2 cases, free 3 cases or more
en primeur Bordeaux, Burgundy. G T
✪ *Clarets at bargain prices – in fact wines from all over France, including plenty of vins de pays. Among other countries New Zealand looks promising, and there's a great range of sherries.*

Connolly's Wine Merchants

Arch 13, 220 Livery Street, Birmingham B3 1EU (0121) 236 9269/3837
fax (0121) 233 2339 e-mail sales@connollyswine.co.uk website www.connollyswine.co.uk
hours Mon–Fri 9–5.30, Sat 10–4 cards AmEx, Maestro, MasterCard, Visa
delivery Surcharge outside Birmingham area discounts 10% for cash & carry en primeur Burgundy. G M T
✪ *There's something for everyone here. Burgundy, Bordeaux and the Rhône all look very good; and there are top names from Germany, Italy, Spain and California. Monthly tutored tastings and winemaker dinners.*

The Co-operative Group

head office New Century House, Manchester M60 4ES Freephone 0800 068 6727 for stock details; approx. 3000 licensed stores e-mail customer.relations@co-op.co.uk website www.co-operative.co.uk hours Variable cards Variable.
✪ *Champions of Fairtrade wines. Tasty stuff from South Africa, Australia, Chile and Argentina for around £5.*

Corney & Barrow

head office No. 1 Thomas More Street, London E1W 1YZ (020) 7265 2400 fax (020) 7265 2539
• Corney & Barrow East Anglia, Belvoir House, High Street, Newmarket CB8 8DH (01638) 600000
• Corney & Barrow (Scotland) with Whighams of Ayr, 8 Academy Street, Ayr KA7 1HT (01292) 267000, and Oxenfoord Castle, by Pathhead, Mid Lothian EH37 5UD (01875) 321921
e-mail wine@corneyandbarrow.com website www.corneyandbarrow.com hours Mon–Fri 8–6 (24-hr answering machine); Newmarket Mon–Sat 9–6; Edinburgh Mon–Fri 9–6; Ayr Mon–Fri 10–5.30, Sat 10–5.30 cards AmEx, Maestro, MasterCard, Visa delivery Free for all orders above £200 within mainland UK, otherwise £9 + VAT per delivery. For Scotland and East Anglia, please contact the relevant office en primeur Bordeaux, Burgundy, Champagne, Rhône, Italy, Spain. C G M T

○ *Top names in French and other European wines; Australia, South Africa and South America also impressive. Wines in every price bracket – try them out at Corney & Barrow wine bars in London.*

Croque-en-Bouche
Groom's Cottage, Underdown, Gloucester Road, Ledbury HR8 2JE (01531) 636400
fax 08707 066282 e-mail mail@croque-en-bouche.co.uk website www.croque-en-bouche.co.uk
hours By appointment 7 days a week cards MasterCard, Visa, debit cards discounts 3% for orders over £500 if paid by cheque or debit card delivery Free locally; elsewhere £5 per consignment; free in England and Wales for orders over £500 if paid by credit card minimum order 1 mixed case (12 Items) or £180. M
○ *A wonderful list, including older wines. Mature Australian reds from the 1990s; terrific stuff from the Rhône; some top clarets; and a generous sprinkling from other parts of the world.*

DeFINE Food & Wine
Chester Road, Sandiway, Cheshire CW8 2NH (01606) 882101
fax (01606) 888407 e-mail office@definefoodandwine.com website www.dcfincfoodandwine.com
hours Mon–Sat 10–8; Sun 12–6 cards AmEx, Maestro, MasterCard, Visa discounts 5% off 12 bottles or more
delivery Free locally, otherwise £10 UK minimum order 1 mixed case. C G M T
○ *Wine shop and delicatessen, with British cheeses and handmade pies and food specialities from Italy and Spain. Excellent, wide-ranging list of over 1000 wines including plenty of New World wines, as well as European classics.*

Devigne Wines
211 The Murrays, Edinburgh EH17 8UN (0131) 664 9058
Fax (05600) 756 287 e-mail info@devignewines.co.uk website www.devignewines.co.uk hours Mon–Fri 10–6 (telephone 7 days) cards Maestro, MasterCard, Visa discounts Selected mixed cases at introductory rate
delivery Free for orders over £300, otherwise £6.50 per consignment. M
○ *Small list specializing in French wine: traditional-method sparkling wines from all over France, a wide choice of rosés, Gaillac from the South-West and wines from the Languedoc and the Jura.*

Direct Wine Shipments
5–7 Corporation Square, Belfast, Northern Ireland BT1 3AJ (028) 9050 8000
fax (028) 9050 8004 e-mail shop@directwine.co.uk website www.directwine.co.uk
hours Mon–Fri 9–6.30 (Thur 10–8), Sat 9.30–5.30 cards Delta, Electron, Maestro, MasterCard, Solo, Switch,Visa

discounts 10% in the form of complementary wine with each case delivery Free Northern Ireland 1 case or more, variable delivery charge for UK mainland depending on customer spend en primeur Bordeaux, Burgundy, Rhône. C M T

✪ *Rhône, Spain, Australia and Burgundy outstanding; Italy, Germany and Chile not far behind; there's good stuff from pretty much everywhere. Wine courses, tastings and expert advice offered.*

Nick Dobson Wines

38 Crail Close, Wokingham, Berkshire RG41 2PZ 0800 849 3078

fax 0870 460 2358 e-mail nick.dobson@nickdobsonwines.co.uk website www.nickdobsonwines.co.uk

hours Mon–Sat 9–5 cards Access, Maestro, MasterCard, Visa delivery £7.95 + VAT 1 case; £4.80 + VAT 2nd case and subsequent cases to UK mainland addresses. Free local delivery. M T

✪ *Mail order outfit specializing in wines from Switzerland, Austria and Beaujolais. Burgundy, Germany and New Zealand are also covered in this list. Plenty of wines at under £10.*

Domaine Direct

8 Cynthia Street, London N1 9JF (020) 7837 1142

fax (020) 7837 8605 e-mail mail@domainedirect.co.uk website www.domainedirect.co.uk

hours 8.30–6 or answering machine cards Maestro, MasterCard, Visa delivery Free London; elsewhere in UK mainland 1 case £13.75, 2 cases £21, 3 cases £23.50, 4 or more free minimum order 1 mixed case en primeur Burgundy. M T

✪ *Sensational Burgundy list; prices are very reasonable for the quality. Also the Burgundian-style Chardonnays from Australia's Leeuwin Estate.*

Farr Vintners

220 Queenstown Road, Battersea, London SW8 4LP (020) 7821 2000

fax (020) 7821 2020 e-mail sales@farrvintners.com website www.farrvintners.com

hours Mon–Fri 9–6 cards Access, Maestro, Mastercard, Visa delivery London £1 per case (min £15); elsewhere at cost minimum order £500 + VAT en primeur Bordeaux. C M T

✪ *A fantastic list of the world's finest wines. The majority is Bordeaux, but you'll also find top stuff and older vintages of white Burgundy, red Rhône, plus Italy, Australia and California.*

Fine Wines of New Zealand

mail order (020) 7482 0093 fax (020) 7267 8400 e-mail sales@fwnz.co.uk or info@fwnz.co.uk

website www.fwnz.co.uk (to place an order contact Catchpole & Froggitt freephone 0800 0856186 or

www.pullthecork.com) hours Mon–Fri 9–6 delivery Free minimum order 1 unmixed case. M
✪ *There are some great names from New Zealand, including Ata Rangi, Pegasus Bay, Redwood Valley and Stonyridge.*

Fingal-Rock
64 Monnow Street, Monmouth NP25 3EN
tel & fax 01600 712372 e-mail tom@pinotnoir.co.uk website www.pinotnoir.co.uk
hours Mon 9.30–1.30, Thurs & Fri 9.30–5.30, Sat 9.30–5 cards Maestro, MasterCard, Visa discounts 5% for at least
12 bottles collected from shop, 7.5% for collected orders over £500, 10% for collected orders over £1200
delivery Free locally (within 30 miles); orders further afield free if over £100. G M T
✪ *The list's great strength is Burgundy, from some very good growers and priced between £6 and £40. Small but tempting
selections from other French regions, as well as Italy, Spain, Portugal and the New World.*

Flagship Wines
417 Hatfield Road, St Albans, Hertfordshire AL4 0XP (01727) 865309 e-mail sales@flagshipwines.co.uk
website www.flagshipwines.co.uk hours Tues–Thurs 11–6, Fri 11–7.30, Sat 10–6 cards AmEx, Maestro, MasterCard,
Visa delivery Free to St Albans addresses and £8 to other UK mainland addresses. G M T
✪ *Well-run independent whose prices can match those of the supermarkets – and you get the friendly, well-informed
advice of boss Julia Jenkins thrown in. Some interesting Italians but strongest in Spain, Australia and Portugal.*

Le Fleming Wines
mail order 19 Spenser Road, Harpenden, Hertfordshire AL5 5NW (01582) 760125
e-mail cherry@leflemingwines.co.uk website www.leflemingwines.co.uk hours 24-hour answering machine discounts
5% on large orders delivery Free locally minimum order 1 case. G
✪ *Mainly New World and France, and short, focused selections from Italy and Spain.*

The Flying Corkscrew
Leighton Buzzard Road, Water End, Nr Hemel Hempstead, Hertfordshire HP1 3BD (01442) 412311
fax (01442) 412313 e-mail sales@flyingcorkscrew.co.uk website www.flyingcorkscrew.co.uk
hours Mon–Wed 10–7, Thurs–Fri 10–8, Sat 10–6, Sun 11–4 cards AmEx, Maestro, MasterCard, Visa
discounts 10% on case delivery Free for orders over £100; £10 per case under £100. G M T
✪ *The list is overflowing with an extensive and imaginative range of wines from every corner of France. Italy, Australia and
the US are terrific. Friendly, knowledgeable staff – and if you're local, look out for tastings led by experts and winemakers.*

Fortnum & Mason

181 Piccadilly, London W1A 1ER (020) 7734 8040

fax (020) 7437 3278 ordering line 0845 300 1707 e-mail info@fortnumandmason.co.uk
website www.fortnumandmason.com hours Mon–Sat 10–6.30, Sun 12–6 (Food Hall and Patio Restaurant only)
cards AmEx, Diners, Maestro, MasterCard, Visa discounts 1 free bottle per unmixed dozen
delivery £7 per delivery address en primeur Bordeaux. M T

✪ *Impressive names from just about everywhere, including Champagne, Bordeaux, Burgundy, Italy, Germany, Australia, New Zealand, South Africa and California. Impeccably sourced own-label range.*

Friarwood

26 New King's Road, London SW6 4ST (020) 7736 2628 fax (020) 7731 0411
• 16 Dock Street, Leith, Edinburgh, EH6 6EY (0131) 554 4159 fax (0131) 554 6703 e-mail sales@friarwood.com; edinburgh@friarwood.com website www.friarwood.com hours Mon–Sat 10–7
cards AmEx, Diners, Maestro, MasterCard, Visa, Solo, Electron discounts 5% on mixed cases, 10% unmixed
delivery (London) Free within M25 and on orders over £250 in mainland UK; (Edinburgh) free locally and for 2 cases or more elsewhere (under 2 cases at cost) en primeur Bordeaux. C G M T

✪ *The focus is Bordeaux, including mature wines from a good selection of petits châteaux as well as classed growths. Burgundy and other French regions are strong too.*

Gauntleys

4 High Street, Exchange Arcade, Nottingham NG1 2ET (0115) 911 0555
fax (0115) 911 0557 e-mail rhône@gauntleywine.com website www.gauntleywine.com
hours Mon–Sat 9–5.30 cards Maestro, MasterCard, Visa delivery Free within Nottingham area, otherwise 1 case £10.95, 2–3 cases £9.50, 4 or more cases free minimum order 1 case en primeur Alsace, Burgundy, Italy, Loire, Rhône, southern France, Spain. M T

✪ *They've won awards for their Rhône and Alsace lists. The Loire, Burgundy, southern France and Spain are also excellent.*

Goedhuis & Co

6 Rudolf Place, Miles Street, London SW8 1RP (020) 7793 7900
fax (020) 7793 7170 e-mail sales@goedhuis.com website www.goedhuis.com
hours Mon–Fri 9–5.30 cards Maestro, MasterCard, Visa delivery Free 3 cases or more, otherwise £15 England, elsewhere at cost minimum order 1 unmixed case en primeur Bordeaux, Burgundy, Rhône. C G M T

❍ *Fine wine specialist. Bordeaux, Burgundy and the Rhône are the core of the list, but everything is good.*

Great Northern Wine

The Warehouse, Blossomgate, Ripon, North Yorkshire HG4 2AJ (01765) 606767
fax (01765) 609151 e-mail info@greatnorthernwine.co.uk website www.greatnorthernwine.co.uk
hours Tues–Fri 9–6, Sat 9–5.30 cards AmEx, Maestro, MasterCard, Visa discounts 10% on case quantities
delivery Free locally, elsewhere at cost en primeur Bordeaux. G M T
❍ *Particular strengths here are Spain, New Zealand and South America.*

Great Western Wine

The Wine Warehouse, Wells Road, Bath BA2 3AP (01225) 322810 (enquiries) or (01225) 322820 (orders)
fax (01225) 442139 e-mail wine@greatwesternwine.co.uk website www.greatwesternwine.co.uk
hours Mon–Fri 10–7, Sat 10–6 cards AmEx, Maestro, MasterCard, Visa discounts 5% off mixed cases, 8% off unsplit
cases delivery £8.95, free over £200 minimum order 1 mixed case en primeur Australia, Bordeaux, Burgundy, Rioja.
C G M T
❍ *Wide-ranging list, bringing in wines from individual growers around the world. Also organizes events and tastings.*

Peter Green & Co

37A/B Warrender Park Road, Edinburgh EH9 1HJ (0131) 229 5925
fax (0131) 229 0606 e-mail shop@petergreenwines.com hours Tues–Thur 10–6.30, Fri 10–7.30, Sat 10–6.30
cards Maestro, MasterCard, Visa discounts 5% on unmixed half-dozens delivery Free in Edinburgh
minimum order (For delivery) 1 case. G T
❍ *Extensive and adventurous list: Tunisia, India and the Lebanon rub shoulders with France, Italy and Germany.*

Green & Blue

36–38 Lordship Lane, East Dulwich, London, SE22 8HJ (020) 8693 9250
● 20–26 Bedford Road, Clapham, London SW4 7HJ (020) 7498 9648
fax (020) 8693 9260 e-mail info@greenandbluewines.com website www.greenandbluewines.com
hours Dulwich shop: Mon–Fri 10–10, Sat 9–11, Sun 12–10; Dulwich bar: Mon–Sat 9–12, Sun 12–11; Clapham
Mon–Thur 7–11, Fri 7–1, Sat 9–1, Sun 11–11pm cards Delta, Maestro, MasterCard, Visa
discounts 5% off mixed cases (for collection only), 10% on unmixed cases delivery Free locally over £200, otherwise
£10 within M25; elsewhere £10 per case. G T

○ *A tempting list full of unusual, intriguing wines you really want to drink – and you can try them on the spot, in the wine bar, which serves tapas-style food. The staff are knowledgeable, and there's a waiting list for the popular tutored tastings. A new shop attached to the Clapham bar opened in spring 2008.*

Haddows See Thresher Group.

Halifax Wine Company

18 Prescott Street, Halifax, West Yorkshire HX1 2LG (01422) 256333

e-mail andy@halifaxwinecompany.com website www.halifaxwinecompany.com hours Tues & Wed 9–5, Thur & Fri 9–6, Sat 9–5. Closed first week in January and first week in August. cards Access, Maestro, MasterCard, Visa discounts 8% on 12 bottles or more for personal callers to the shop delivery Free in West Yorkshire on orders over £75; rest of UK mainland £9.95 for first 12 bottles then £4.95 per subsequent case. **G M T**

○ *Exciting, wide-ranging and award-winning list.*

Handford Wines

105 Old Brompton Road, South Kensington, London SW7 3LE (020) 7589 6113 fax (020) 7581 2983

e-mail jack@handford.net website www.handford.net hours Mon–Sat 10–8.30 cards AmEx, MasterCard, Visa discounts 5% on mixed cases delivery £8.25 for orders under £150 within UK en primeur Bordeaux, Burgundy. **G M T**

○ *Delightful London shop, absolutely packed with the sort of wines I really want to drink.*

Roger Harris Wines

Loke Farm, Weston Longville, Norfolk NR9 5LG (01603) 880171

fax (01603) 880291 e-mail sales@rogerharriswines.co.uk website www.rogerharriswines.co.uk

hours Mon–Fri 9–5 cards AmEx, MasterCard, Visa delivery Next working day UK mainland, £3 for orders up to £110, £2 up to £160, free over £160 minimum order 1 mixed case. **M**

○ *Britain's acknowledged experts in Beaujolais also have a good range of whites from the neighbouring Mâconnais region.*

Harvey Nichols

109–125 Knightsbridge, London SW1X 7RJ (020) 7235 5000

• The Mailbox, 31–32 Wharfside Street, Birmingham B1 1RE (0121) 616 6000

• 30–34 St Andrew Square, Edinburgh EH2 2AD (0131) 524 8388

• 107–111 Briggate, Leeds LS1 6AZ (0113) 204 8888

- 21 New Cathedral Street, Manchester M1 1AD (0161) 828 8888

e-mail wineshop@harveynichols.com website www.harveynichols.com

hours (London) Mon–Fri 10–8, Sat 10–7, Sun 12–6; (Birmingham) Mon–Wed 10–6, Thurs 10–8, Fri–Sat 10–7, Sun 11–5; (Edinburgh) Mon–Wed 10–6, Thurs 10–8, Fri, Sat 10–7, Sun 11–5; (Leeds) Mon–Wed 10–6, Thurs–Fri 10–7, Sat 9–7, Sun 12–6; (Manchester) Mon, Wed, Fri 10–7, Thurs 10–8, Sat 9–7, Sun 12–6

cards AmEx, Maestro, MasterCard, Visa.

✪ *Sought-after producers and cult fine wines, especially from France, Italy and California.*

Haynes Hanson & Clark

Sheep Street, Stow-on-the-Wold, Gloucestershire GL54 1AA (01451) 870808 fax (01451) 870508

- 7 Elystan Street, London SW3 3NT (020) 7584 7927 fax (020) 7584 7967

e-mail stow@hhandc.co.uk or london@hhandc.co.uk website www.hhandc.co.uk

hours (Stow) Mon–Fri 9–6, Sat 9–5.30; (London) Mon–Fri 9–7, Sat 9–4.30 cards Access, Maestro, MasterCard, Visa discounts 10% unsplit case delivery Free central London and Gloucestershire for 1 case or more; elsewhere 1 case £14.50, 2–3 cases £8.90 per case, 4 or more cases £7.25 per case, free orders for over £650

en primeur Bordeaux, Burgundy. M T

✪ *Known for its subtle, elegant wines: top-notch Burgundy is the main focus of the list, but other French regions are well represented, and there's interesting stuff from Spain, Italy, Australia and New Zealand.*

Hedley Wright

11 Twyford Centre, London Road, Bishop's Stortford, Herts CM23 3YT (01279) 465818 fax (01279) 465819

- Wyevale Garden Centre, Cambridge Road, Hitchin, Herts, SG4 0JT (01462) 431110 fax (01462) 422983

e-mail sales@hedleywright.co.uk website www.hedleywright.co.uk hours Mon–Wed 9–6, Thur–Fri 9–7, Sat 10–6; (Hitchin) Mon–Wed 11–7, Thur–Fri 11–8, Sat 11–7, Sun 11–5 cards AmEx, Maestro, MasterCard, Visa delivery £5 per delivery, free for orders over £100 minimum order 1 mixed case en primeur Bordeaux, Chile, Germany, Port. C G M T

✪ *A good all-round list, especially strong on France and Italy.*

Hicks & Don

4 Old Station Yard, Edington, Westbury, Wiltshire BA13 4NT (01380) 831234 fax (01380) 831010

- Park House, North Elmham, Dereham, Norfolk NR20 5JY (01362) 668571 fax (01362) 668573

e-mail mailbox@hicksanddon.co.uk website www.hicksanddon.co.uk hours Mon–Fri 9–5

cards Maestro, MasterCard, Visa discounts Negotiable delivery Free over £100, otherwise £6 per case minimum order 1 case en primeur Bordeaux, Burgundy, Chile, Italy, Port, Rhône. C G M T

✪ *Subtle, well-made wines that go with food and plenty of good-value wines at around £6 for everyday drinking.*

Jeroboams (incorporating Laytons)

head office 7–9 Elliot's Place, London N1 8HX (020) 7288 8888 fax (020) 7359 2616

shops 50–52 Elizabeth Street, London SW1W 9PB (020) 7730 8108

- 20 Davies Street, London W1K 3DT (020) 7499 1015
- 96 Holland Park Avenue, London W11 3RB (020) 7727 9359
- 6 Pont Street, London SW1X 9EL (020) 7235 1612
- 29 Heath Street, London NW3 6TR (020) 7435 6845
- 56 Walton Street, London SW3 1RB (020) 7589 2020
- 1 St. John's Wood High Street, London NW8 7NG (020) 7722 4020
- 13 Elgin Crescent, London W11 2JA (020) 7229 0527
- Mr Christian's Delicatessen, 11 Elgin Crescent, London W11 2JA (020) 7229 0501
- Milroy's of Soho, 3 Greek Street, London W1D 4NX (020) 7437 2385 (whisky and wine)

e-mail sales@jeroboams.co.uk website www.jeroboams.co.uk hours Offices Mon–Fri 9–6, shops Mon–Sat 9–7 (may vary) cards AmEx, Maestro, MasterCard, Visa delivery Free delivery for orders over £200, otherwise £9.95 en primeur Bordeaux, Burgundy, Rhône. C G M T

✪ *Wide-ranging list of affordable and enjoyable wines, especially good in France, Italy, Australia and New Zealand. Fine foods, especially cheeses and olive oils, are available in the Holland Park and Mr Christian's Delicatessen shops.*

S H Jones

27 High Street, Banbury, Oxfordshire OX16 5EW (01295) 251179 fax (01295) 272352 e-mail banbury@shjones.com

- 9 Market Square, Bicester, Oxfordshire OX26 6AA (01869) 322448 e-mail bicester@shjones.com
- The Cellar Shop, 2 Riverside, Tramway Road, Banbury, Oxfordshire OX16 5TU (01295) 672296 fax (01295) 259560 e-mail retail@shjones.com
- 121 Regent Street, Leamington Spa, Warwickshire CV32 4NU (01926) 315609 e-mail leamington@shjones.com

website www.shjones.com hours Please call each store for details cards Maestro, MasterCard, Visa delivery Free for 12 bottles of wine/spirits or total value over £100 within 15-mile radius of shops, otherwise £9.75 per case en primeur Bordeaux, Burgundy, Port. C G M T

✪ *Wide-ranging list with good Burgundies and Rhônes, clarets from under a tenner to top names and plenty of tasty stuff from elsewhere – southern France to South America. There is now a wine bar at the High Street shop in Banbury.*

Justerini & Brooks

mail order 61 St James's Street, London SW1A 1LZ (020) 7484 6400 fax (020) 7484 6499
e-mail justorders@justerinis.com website www.justerinis.com hours Mon–Fri 9–5.30
cards Maestro, MasterCard, Visa delivery Free for unmixed cases over £250, otherwise £15 UK mainland minimum
order 1 case en primeur Alsace, Bordeaux, Burgundy, Italy, Loire, Rhône, Germany. C M T
✪ *Superb list of top-quality wines from Europe's classic regions, as well as some excellent New World choices. While some
wines are very pricy, there is plenty for less than a tenner*

Laithwaites

mail order New Aquitaine House, Exeter Way, Theale, Reading, Berkshire RG7 4PL order line 0845 444 8282
fax 0870 444 8182 e-mail orders@laithwaites.co.uk website www.laithwaites.co.uk hours Mon–Fri 8–11, Sat–Sun
8–9 cards AmEx, Diners, Maestro, MasterCard, Visa discounts On unmixed cases of 6 or 12 delivery £5.99 per order
en primeur Australia, Bordeaux, Burgundy, Rhône, Rioja. C M T
✪ *Extensive selection of wines from France, Australia, Spain, Italy and elsewhere. Informative website offers excellent mixed
cases, while the bin ends and special offers are good value.*

Lay & Wheeler

Holton Park, Holton St Mary, Suffolk CO7 6NN 0845 330 1855 fax 0845 330 4095
e-mail sales@laywheeler.com website www.laywheeler.com
hours (Order office) Mon–Fri 8.30–5.30, Sat 9–1 cards Maestro, MasterCard, Visa delivery £9.95; free for orders over
£200 en primeur Bordeaux, Burgundy, Port (some vintages), Rhône, Spain. C M T
• Wheeler Cellars, 117 Gosbecks Park, Colchester, Essex CO2 9JJ (01206) 713560 fax (01206) 769552
e-mail wheeler.cellars@laywheeler.com C G M T
✪ *First-class Bordeaux and Burgundy to satisfy the most demanding drinker, and plenty more besides. A must-have list.*

Laymont & Shaw

The Old Chapel, Millpool, Truro, Cornwall TR1 1EX (01872) 270545 fax (01872) 223005
e-mail info@laymont-shaw.co.uk website www.laymont-shaw.co.uk hours Mon–Fri 9–5 cards Maestro, MasterCard,
Visa discounts £5 per case if wines collected, also £1 per case for 2 cases, £2 for 3–5, £3 for 6 or more
delivery Free UK mainland minimum order 1 mixed case. C G M T
✪ *Excellent, knowledgeable list that specializes in Spain, with something from just about every region.*

Lea & Sandeman

170 Fulham Road, London SW10 9PR (020) 7244 0522 fax (020) 7244 0533

• 211 Kensington Church Street, London W8 7LX (020) 7221 1982

• 51 High Street, Barnes, London SW13 9LN (020) 8878 8643 e-mail info@leaandsandeman.co.uk
website www.londonfinewine.co.uk hours Mon–Sat 10–8 cards AmEx, Maestro, MasterCard, Visa
discounts 5–15% by case, other discounts on 10 cases or more delivery London £10 for less than £100, otherwise free,
and to UK mainland south of Perth on orders over £250 en primeur Bordeaux, Burgundy, Italy. C G M T
✪ *Burgundy and Italy take precedence here, and there's a succession of excellent names, chosen with great care. Bordeaux
has wines at all price levels, and there are short but fascinating ranges from the USA, Spain, Australia and New Zealand.*

Liberty Wines

mail order Unit D18, New Covent Garden Food Market, London SW8 5LL (020) 7720 5350
fax (020) 7720 6158 website www.libertywine.co.uk e-mail info@libertywine.co.uk hours Mon–Fri 9–5.30
cards Maestro, MasterCard, Visa delivery Free to mainland UK minimum order 1 mixed case. M
✪ *Italy rules, with superb wines from pretty well all the best producers. Liberty are the UK agents for most of their
producers, so if you're interested in Italian wines, this should be your first port of call. Also top names from Australia
and elsewhere.*

Linlithgow Wines

Crossford, Station Road, Linlithgow, West Lothian EH49 6BW tel & fax (01506) 848821
e-mail jrobmcd@aol.com hours Mon–Fri 9–5.30 (please phone first) cards None: cash, cheque or bank transfer
only delivery Free locally; elsewhere in UK £9 for 1 case, £7 per case for 2 or more. G M T
✪ *Specialist in the south of France – Languedoc, southern Rhône and Provence – with lots around £5–7; prices rarely
exceed £20.*

O W Loeb & Co

3 Archie Street, off Tanner Street, London SE1 3JT (020) 7234 0385
fax (020) 7357 0440 e-mail finewine@owloeb.com website www.owloeb.com hours Mon–Fri 8.30–5.30
cards Maestro, MasterCard, Visa discounts 3 cases and above delivery Free 3 cases or more and on orders over £250
minimum order 1 case en primeur Burgundy, Bordeaux, Rhône, Germany (Mosel). C M T
✪ *Burgundy, the Rhône, Loire and Germany stand out, with top producers galore. Then there are Loeb's new discoveries
from Spain and the New World, especially New Zealand and South Africa.*

Maison du Vin

Moor Hill, Hawkhurst, Kent TN18 4PF (01580) 753487

fax (01580) 755627 e-mail kvgriffin@aol.com website www.maison-du-vin.co.uk hours Mon 10–4, Tue and Thu 10–8, Wed and Fri 10–5, Sat 10–6 cards Access, AmEx, Maestro, MasterCard, Visa delivery Free locally; UK mainland at cost en primeur Bordeaux. C G M T

✪ *As the name suggests, the focus is on French wines, at prices from about £6 upwards. There's a monthly themed 'wine school' or you can book personal tutored tastings.*

Majestic

(see also Wine and Beer World page 189)

head office Majestic House, Otterspool Way, Watford, Herts WD25 8WW (01923) 298200

fax (01923) 819105; 136 stores nationwide e-mail info@majestic.co.uk website www.majestic.co.uk

hours Mon–Fri 10–8, Sat 9–7, Sun 10–5 (may vary) cards AmEx, Diners, Maestro, MasterCard, Visa

delivery Free UK mainland minimum order 1 mixed case (12 bottles) en primeur Bordeaux, Port, Burgundy. G M T

✪ *One of the best places to buy Champagne, with a good range and good discounts for buying in quantity. Loads of interesting and reasonably priced stuff, especially from France and the New World.*

Marks & Spencer

head office Waterside House, 35 North Wharf Road, London W2 1NW (020) 7935 4422

fax (020) 7487 2679; 600 licensed stores website www.marksandspencer.com hours Variable discounts Variable, a selection of 10 different Wines of the Month available, buy any 6 and save 10% in selected stores. M T

✪ *M&S works with top producers around the world to create its impressive list of own-label wines. All the wines are exclusive and unique to M&S, selected and blended by their in-house winemaking team.*

Martinez Wines

35 The Grove, Ilkley, Leeds, West Yorkshire LS29 9NJ (01943) 600000

fax 0870 922 3940 e-mail julian@martinez.co.uk website www.martinez.co.uk

hours Sun 12–6, Mon–Wed 10–8, Thurs–Fri 10–9, Sat 9.30–6 cards AmEx, Maestro, MasterCard, Visa

discounts 5% on 6 bottles or more, 10% off orders over £150 delivery Free local delivery, otherwise £11 per case mainland UK en primeur Bordeaux, Burgundy. C G M T

✪ *Carefully chosen selection – Alsace and Beaujolais look spot-on, as do Bordeaux, Burgundy and Rhône, so I would trust their selection from other regions.*

Millésima

87 Quai de Paludate, BP 89, 33038 Bordeaux Cedex, France (00 33) 5 57 80 88 08

fax (00 33) 5 57 80 88 19 Freephone 0800 917 0352 website www.millesima.com hours Mon–Fri 8–5.30 cards AmEx, Diners, Maestro, MasterCard, Visa delivery For bottled wines, free to single UK addresses for orders exceeding £500. Otherwise, a charge of £20 will be applied. For en primeur wines, free to single UK addresses. en primeur Bordeaux, Burgundy, Rhône. C M T

✪ *Wine comes direct from the châteaux to Millésima's cellars, where 3 million bottles are stored. A sprinkling of established names from other French regions.*

Montrachet

mail order 59 Kennington Road, London SE1 7PZ (020) 7928 1990

fax (020) 7928 3415 e-mail andy@montrachetwine.com website www.montrachetwine.com hours (Office and mail order) Mon–Fri 8.30–5.30 cards Maestro, MasterCard, Visa delivery England and Wales £12 including VAT, free for 3 or more cases; for Scotland ring for details minimum order 1 unmixed case en primeur Bordeaux, Burgundy. M T

✪ *Impressive Burgundies are the main attraction here, but there are also some very good Rhônes, and Bordeaux is excellent at all price levels.*

Moreno Wines

11 Marylands Road, London W9 2DU (020) 7286 0678

fax (020) 7286 0513 e-mail merchant@moreno-wines.co.uk website www.morenowinedirect.com hours Mon–Fri 4–9, Sat 12–9 cards AmEx, Maestro, MasterCard, Visa discounts 10% 2 or more cases delivery Free locally, 3 or more cases within UK also free, otherwise £7.50. M T

✪ *Specialist in Spanish wines, some fine and rare, with prices to match, but plenty of everyday drinking too, including whites and rosados.*

Wm Morrisons Supermarkets

head office Hilmore House, Gain Lane, Bradford, West Yorkshire BD3 7DL 0845 611 5000

fax 0845 611 6801 customer service 0845 611 6111; 371 licensed branches website www.morrisons.co.uk hours Variable, generally Mon–Sat 8–8, Sun 10–4 cards AmEx, Delta, Maestro, MasterCard, Solo, Style, Visa Electron. G T

✪ *Inexpensive, often tasty wines, and if you're prepared to trade up a little there's some really good stuff here.*

James Nicholson

7/9 Killyleagh Street, Crossgar, Co. Down, Northern Ireland BT30 9DQ (028) 4483 0091
fax (028) 4483 0028 e-mail shop@jnwine.com website www.jnwine.com hours Mon–Sat 10–7
cards Maestro, MasterCard, Visa discounts 10% mixed case delivery Free (1 case or more) in Eire and Northern
Ireland; UK mainland £10.95, 2 cases £5.95 en primeur Bordeaux, Burgundy, California, Rioja, Rhône. C G M T
✪ *Well-chosen list mainly from small, committed growers around the world. Bordeaux, Rhône and southern France are
slightly ahead of the field, there's a good selection of Burgundy and some excellent drinking from Germany and Spain.*

Nickolls & Perks

37 Lower High Street, Stourbridge, West Midlands DY8 1TA (01384) 394518
fax (01384) 440786 e-mail sales@nickollsandperks.co.uk website www.nickollsandperks.co.uk
hours Tues–Fri 10.30–5.30, Sat 10.30–5 cards Maestro, MasterCard, Visa discounts negotiable per case
delivery £10 per consignment en primeur Bordeaux, Champagne, Port. C G M T
✪ *Established in 1797, Nickolls & Perks have a wide-ranging list – and a terrific website – covering most areas.
Their strength is France. Advice is available to clients wishing to develop their cellars or invest in wine.*

Nidderdale Fine Wines

2a High Street, Pateley Bridge, North Yorkshire HG3 5AW (01423) 711703
e-mail info@southaustralianwines.com website www.southaustralianwines.com hours Mon–Sat 10–6 cards Maestro,
MasterCard, Visa discounts 5% case discount on shop purchases delivery £7.50 per case in England, Wales and
southern Scotland. Single bottle delivery available. G T
✪ *Specialist in South Australia, with 300 wines broken down into regions. Also 350 or so wines from other parts
of Australia and the rest of the world. Look out for online offers and winemaker dinners.*

Noble Rot Wine Warehouses

18 Market Street, Bromsgrove, Worcestershire, B61 8DA (01527) 575606 fax (01527) 833133
e-mail info@noble-rot.co.uk website www.noble-rot.co.uk hours Tues–Fri 10–6.30, Sat & Mon 9.30–5.30
cards Maestro, MasterCard, Visa discounts Various delivery Free within 10-mile radius. G T
✪ *Australia, Italy, France and Spain feature strongly in a frequently changing list of more than 400 wines, mostly at
£5–£15.*

The following services are available where indicated: C = cellarage **G** = glass hire/loan **M** = mail/online order **T** = tastings and talks

The Nobody Inn

Doddiscombsleigh, Nr Exeter, Devon EX6 7PS (01647) 252394

fax (01647) 252978 e-mail info@nobodyinn.co.uk website www.nobodyinn.co.uk hours Mon–Sun 12–3 & 6–11 (summer)
cards AmEx, Maestro, MasterCard, Visa discounts 5% per case delivery £7.99 for 1 case, free over £150. G M T
• The Nobody Wine Company (01647) 252394 fax (01647) 252978 e-mail sales@thenobodywinecompany.co.uk
website www.thenobodywinecompany.co.uk hours 24-hr ordering service delivery Free for orders over £150.
❂ *The 16th-century Nobody Inn has an extraordinary list of more than 700 wines. Australia rules, but there's something
exciting from just about everywhere. The Wine Company is a mail-order venture for wines mostly priced at £5–10.*

O'Briens

head office 33 Spruce Avenue, Stillorgan Industrial Park, Co. Dublin, Ireland (low cost number) 1850 269 777
fax 01 2697480; 27 stores e-mail sales@obrienswines.ie; info@obrienswines.ie website www.wine.ie
hours Mon–Sat 10am–11pm, Sun 1–11pm cards MasterCard, Visa delivery 10 per case anywhere in Ireland (minimum
order 6 bottles); free for orders over 200 en primeur Bordeaux. G M T
❂ *Family-owned drinks retailer, which could well claim to be the best of the chains in Ireland. Imports directly from over 75
wineries worldwide.*

Oddbins

head office 31–33 Weir Road, London SW19 8UG (020) 8944 4400
fax (020) 8944 4411 mail order Oddbins Direct 0800 328 2323 fax 0800 328 3848; 173 shops nationwide
website www.oddbins.com hours Ask local branch for details cards AmEx, Maestro, MasterCard, Visa
discounts 6 for 5 on Champagne or sparkling wine; 10% off 6 bottles or 20% off 12 bottles of table wine, excluding fine
wine; regular general promotions delivery (Stores) free locally for orders over £100 en primeur Bordeaux. G M T
• Calais store Cité Europe, 139 Rue de Douvres, 62901, Coquelles Cedex, France (0033) 3 21 82 07 32
fax (0033) 3 21 82 05 83 pre-order www.oddbins.com/storefinder/calais.asp
❂ *New World meets the classic regions of Europe: extensive Aussie selection, well-chosen Chileans, Argentinians and South
Africans sit alongside good stuff from all over France, Spain and Italy. Always a good choice of fizz.*

The Oxford Wine Company

The Wine Warehouse, Witney Road, Standlake, Oxon OX29 7PR (01865) 301144
fax (01865) 301155 e-mail info@oxfordwine.co.uk website www.oxfordwine.co.uk
hours Mon–Sat 9–7, Sun 11–4 cards AmEx, Diners, Maestro, MasterCard, Visa discounts 5% discount on a case of 12,

no minimum order delivery Free locally; national delivery £9.99 for any amount en primeur Bordeaux. G M T
✪ *A good selection from the classic regions and the New World, from bargain basement prices to expensive fine wines. Easy-to-use website. They also organize tastings and other events.*

OZ WINES
mail order Freepost Lon 17656, London SW18 5BR, 0845 450 1261
fax (020) 8870 8839 e-mail sales@ozwines.co.uk website www.ozwines.co.uk hours Mon–Fri 9.30–7
cards Access, Diners, Maestro, MasterCard, Visa delivery Free minimum order 1 mixed case. M T
✪ *Australian wines made by small wineries and real people – with the thrilling flavours that Australians do better than anyone.*

Penistone Court Wine Cellars
The Railway Station, Penistone, Sheffield, South Yorkshire S36 6HP (01226) 766037
fax (01226) 767310 e-mail chris@pcwine.plus.com website www.pcwine.co.uk hours Tues–Fri 10–6, Sat 10–3
cards Maestro, MasterCard, Visa delivery Free locally, rest of UK mainland charged at cost 1 case or more
minimum order 1 case. G M
✪ *A well-balanced list, with something from just about everywhere, mostly from familiar names.*

Philglas & Swiggot
21 Northcote Road, Battersea, London SW11 1NG (020) 7924 4494
• 64 Hill Rise, Richmond, London TW10 6UB (020) 8332 6031
• 22 New Quebec Street, Marylebone, London W1H 7SB (020) 7402 0002
e-mail info@philglas-swiggot.co.uk website www.philglas-swiggot.co.uk hours (Battersea and Richmond) Mon–Sat
11–7, Sun 12–5; (Marylebone) Mon–Sat 11–7 cards AmEx, Maestro, MasterCard, Visa discounts 5% per case
delivery Free 1 case locally. G M
✪ *Excellent selections from Australia, Italy, France and Austria – subtle, interesting wines, not blockbuster brands.*

Christopher Piper Wines
1 Silver Street, Ottery St Mary, Devon EX11 1DB (01404) 814139
fax (01404) 812100 e-mail sales@christopherpiperwines.co.uk website www.christopherpiperwines.co.uk
hours Mon–Fri 8.30–5.30, Sat 9–4.30 cards Maestro, MasterCard, Visa discounts 5% mixed case, 10% 3 or more
cases delivery £8.95 for 1 case then £4.80 for each case, free for orders over £220 minimum order (for mail order) 1
mixed case en primeur Bordeaux, Burgundy, Rhône. C G M T

✪ *Huge range of well-chosen wines that reflect a sense of place and personality, with lots of information to help you make up your mind.*

Terry Platt Wine Merchants

Council Street West, Llandudno LL30 1ED (01492) 874099

fax (01492) 874788 e-mail info@terryplattwines.co.uk website www.terryplattwines.co.uk

hours Mon–Fri 8.30–5.30 cards Access, Maestro, MasterCard, Visa delivery Free locally and UK mainland 5 cases or more minimum order 1 mixed case. G M T

✪ *A wide-ranging list with a sprinkling of good growers from most regions. New World coverage has increased recently.*

Playford Ros

Middle Park, Thirsk, Yorkshire YO7 3AH (01845) 526777

fax (01845) 526888 e-mail sales@playfordros.com website www.playfordros.com

hours Mon–Fri 8–6 cards MasterCard, Visa discounts negotiable delivery Free Yorkshire, Derbyshire, Durham, Newcastle; elsewhere £10–15 or at courier cost minimum order 1 mixed case en primeur Bordeaux, Burgundy. G M T

✪ *A carefully chosen list, with reassuringly recognizable Burgundy, exceptional Australian and good stuff from other French regions, Chile, Oregon and New Zealand. Plenty at the £6–8 mark.*

Portland Wine Co

152a Ashley Road, Hale WA15 9SA (0161) 928 0357

fax (0161) 905 1291 e-mail enquiries@portlandwine.co.uk website www.portlandwine.co.uk

hours Mon–Fri 10–9, Sat 9–9 cards Maestro, MasterCard, Visa discounts 5% on 2 cases or more, 10% on 5 cases or more delivery Free locally, £15 + VAT per consignment nationwide, no minimum order en primeur Bordeaux. C T

✪ *Spain, Portugal and Burgundy are specialities and there's a promising-looking list of clarets. Consumer-friendly list with something at every price level from around the world.*

Quaff Fine Wine Merchant

139–141 Portland Road, Hove BN3 5QJ (01273) 820320

fax (01273) 820326 e-mail sales@quaffit.com website www.quaffit.com hours Mon–Thurs 10–7, Fri–Sat 10–8, Sun 12–7 cards Access, Maestro, MasterCard, Visa discounts 10% mixed case delivery Next working day nationwide, charge depends on order value. C G M T

✪ *Extensive and keenly priced list organized by grape variety rather than country.*

Raeburn Fine Wines

21–23 Comely Bank Road, Edinburgh EH4 1DS (0131) 343 1159
fax (0131) 332 5166 e-mail sales@raeburnfinewines.com website www.raeburnfinewines.com
hours Mon–Sat 9.30–6 cards AmEx, Maestro, MasterCard, Visa discounts 5% unsplit case, 2.5% mixed
delivery Free local area 1 or more cases (usually); elsewhere at cost en primeur Australia, Bordeaux, Burgundy,
California, Germany, Italy, Languedoc-Roussillon, Loire, New Zealand, Rhône. G M T
✪ *Carefully chosen list, mainly from small growers. Burgundy and Loire are specialities, with Italy, Austria and northern
Spain close behind.*

Real Wine Co.

1 Cannon Meadow, Bull Lane, Gerrards Cross, Buckinghamshire SL9 8RE (01753) 885619
e-mail mark@therealwineco.co.uk website www.therealwineco.co.uk cards Delta, Maestro, Mastercard, Visa
delivery £5.99 per order, orders over £250 free minimum order 1 mixed case.
✪ *Owner Mark Hughes has based his list entirely on his personal taste – check it out and see if you agree with his lively
tasting notes. There are plenty of good-value wines, including several rosés.*

Reid Wines

The Mill, Marsh Lane, Hallatrow, Nr Bristol BS39 6EB (01761) 452645 fax (01761) 453642 e-mail reidwines@aol.com
hours Mon–Fri 9–5.30 cards Access, Maestro, MasterCard, Visa (3% charge) delivery Free within 25 miles of Hallatrow
(Bristol), and in central London for orders over 2 cases en primeur Claret. C G M T
✪ *A mix of great old wines, some old duds and splendid current stuff. Italy, USA, Australia, port and Madeira look tremendous.*

Richardson & Sons

26a Lowther Street, Whitehaven, Cumbria CA28 7DG (01946) 65334
e-mail orders@richardsonswines.co.uk website www.richardsonswines.co.uk hours Mon–Sat 10–5.30 cards AmEx,
Delta, Maestro, MasterCard, Visa delivery Free locally. M T
✪ *Focused on reds from Australia, Bordeaux and Burgundy. Join their mailing list to get regular updates.*

Howard Ripley

25 Dingwall Road, London SW18 3AZ (020) 8877 3065
fax (020) 8877 0029 e-mail info@howardripley.com website www.howardripley.com
hours Mon–Fri 9–6, Sat 9–1 cards Maestro, MasterCard, Visa delivery Minimum charge £12.50 + VAT, free UK

mainland on orders over £500 ex-VAT minimum order 1 case en primeur Burgundy, Germany. C M T

○ *A must-have list for serious Burgundy lovers; expensive but not excessive. The German range is also excellent.*

Roberson

348 Kensington High Street, London W14 8NS (020) 7371 2121

fax (020) 7371 4010 e-mail retail@roberson.co.uk website www.robersonwinemerchant.co.uk, www.roberson.co.uk
hours Mon–Sat 10–8, Sun 12–6 cards Access, AmEx, Maestro, MasterCard, Visa discounts mail order 5% on
champagne and spirits, 10% or wine cases delivery Free delivery within London, otherwise £15 per case
en primeur Bordeaux, Port. C G M T

○ *Fine and rare wines, sold by the bottle. All of France is excellent; so is Italy and port.*

The RSJ Wine Company

33 Coin Street, London SE1 9NR (020) 7928 4554

fax (020) 7928 9768 e-mail tom.king@rsj.uk.com website www.rsj.uk.com
hours Mon–Fri 9–6, answering machine at other times cards AmEx, Maestro, MasterCard, Visa delivery Free central
London, minimum 1 case; England and Wales (per case), £14.10 1 case, £10.25 2 cases or more. G M T

○ *A roll-call of great Loire names, and some good Bordeaux.*

Sainsbury's

head office 33 Holborn, London EC1N 2HT (020) 7695 6000

customer service 0800 636262; 800 stores website www.sainsburys.co.uk hours Variable, some 24 hrs, locals
generally Mon–Sat 7–11, Sun 10 or 11–4 cards AmEx, Maestro, MasterCard, Visa discounts 5% for 6 bottles or more.
G M T

• mail order 0800 917 4092 fax 0800 917 4095

• Calais store Sainsbury's, Centre Commercial Auchan, Route de Boulogne, 62100 Calais, France (0033) 3 21 82 38 48
preorder www.sainsburys.co.uk and click on Wine at Calais

○ *A collection to cater for bargain hunters as well as lovers of good-value wine higher up the scale. They've expanded their
Taste the Difference range and got some top producers on board.*

Savage Selection

The Ox House, Market Place, Northleach, Cheltenham, Glos GL54 3EG (01451) 860896
fax (01451) 860996 • The Ox House Shop and Wine Bar at same address (01451) 860680

e-mail wine@savageselection.co.uk website www.savageselection.co.uk hours Office: Mon–Fri 9–6; shop: Tue–Wed 10–7.30, Thur–Fri 10–10, Sat 10–4 cards Maestro, MasterCard, Visa delivery Free locally for orders over £100; elsewhere on UK mainland free for orders over £250: otherwise £11.75 per consignment en primeur Bordeaux. C G M T
✪ *Owner Mark Savage seeks out wines of genuine originality and personality from a wide variety of places, many of them less than mainstream.*

Seckford Wines

Dock Lane, Melton, Suffolk IP12 1PE (01394) 446622
fax (01394) 446633 e-mail sales@seckfordwines.co.uk website www.seckfordwines.co.uk
cards Maestro, MasterCard, Visa delivery £11.75 inc VAT per consignment, UK mainland; elsewhere at cost
minimum order 1 mixed case en primeur Bordeaux, Burgundy. C M
✪ *Bordeaux, Burgundy, Champagne and the Rhône are the stars of this list, with some excellent older vintages. Serious stuff from Italy and Spain, too.*

Selfridges

400 Oxford Street, London W1A 1AB 0800 123 400 (for all stores)
• Upper Mall East, Bullring, Birmingham B5 4BP
• 1 Exchange Square, Manchester M3 1BD
• The Trafford Centre, Manchester M17 8DA
fax (01394) 446633 e-mail wineshop@selfridges.co.uk website www.selfridges.com hours London Mon–Sat 9.30–8 (Thurs –9pm), Sun 11.30–6.15; Birmingham Mon–Sat 10–8 (Thurs –9), Sun 10.30–5; Manchester Exchange Mon–Fri 10–8 (Thurs –9), Sat 9–8, Sun 10.30–5; Manchester Trafford Mon–Sat 10–10 (Thurs –9), Sun 12–6 cards Maestro, MasterCard, Visa discounts 10% case discount delivery next day £10 within UK mainland. T
✪ *Strong fine wine list. Great selection for gifts and regular tastings. Also strong on spirits.*

Somerfield

head office Somerfield House, Whitchurch Lane, Bristol BS14 0TJ (0117) 935 9359
fax (0117) 935 6669; 940 Somerfield stores website www.somerfield.co.uk hours Mon–Sat 8–8, Sun 10–4 cards Maestro, MasterCard, Visa discounts 5% off 6 bottles delivery Free local delivery for orders over £25 in selected stores.
✪ *Wines from all over, ranging from bargain prices to the £25 mark. Lots of choice on New World wines.*

The following services are available where indicated: **C** = cellarage **G** = glass hire/loan **M** = mail/online order **T** = tastings and talks

Sommelier Wine Co. Ltd.

23 St George's Esplanade, St Peter Port, Guernsey, Channel Islands, GY1 2BG (01481) 721677
fax (01481) 716818 hours Mon–Sat 9.15–5.30, except Fri 9.15–6 cards Maestro, MasterCard, Visa
discounts 5% 1 case or more delivery Free locally (minimum 1 mixed case); being outside the European Community and
with Customs restrictions means that the shipping of wine to the UK mainland is not possible. G T
○ *An excellent list, with interesting, unusual wines. A big selection of top-notch Australia, Italy, Loire, Beaujolais, Burgundy,
Bordeaux, the Rhône, Spain and South Africa.*

Stainton Wines

1 Station Yard, Station Road, Kendal, Cumbria LA9 6BT (01539) 731886 fax (01539) 730396
e-mail admin@stainton-wines.co.uk website www.stainton-wines.co.uk hours Mon–Fri 9–5.30, Sat 9–4.30
cards Maestro, MasterCard, Visa discounts 5% mixed case delivery Free Cumbria and North Lancashire;
elsewhere (per case) £13 1 case, more than 1 case variable. G M T
○ *The list includes some great Bordeaux, interesting Burgundy, and leading names from Italy and Chile.*

Stevens Garnier

47 West Way, Botley, Oxford OX2 0JF (01865) 263303
fax (01865) 791594 e-mail shop@stevensgarnier.co.uk hours Mon–Thur 10–6, Fri 10–7, Sat 9.30–5.30
cards AmEx, Maestro, MasterCard, Visa, Solo discounts 5% on a mixed case delivery Free locally. G M T
○ *Regional France is a strength: this is one of the few places in the UK you can buy wine from Savoie. Likewise, there are
interesting choices from Portugal, Australia, Chile and Canada.*

Stone, Vine & Sun

No. 13 Humphrey Farms, Hazeley Road, Twyford, Winchester SO21 1QA (01962) 712351
fax (01962) 717545 e-mail sales@stonevine.co.uk website www.stonevine.co.uk
hours Mon–Fri 9–6, Sat 9.30–4 cards Access, Maestro, MasterCard, Visa discounts 5% on an unmixed case
delivery £5 for 1st case, £8.50 for 2 cases, free for orders over £250. Prices vary for Scottish Highlands, islands
and Northern Ireland. G M T
○ *Lovely list marked by enthusiasm and passion for the subject. Lots of interesting stuff from France, but also from
Germany, South Africa, New Zealand, Chile, Argentina and elsewhere.*

The following services are available where indicated: **C** = cellarage **G** = glass hire/loan **M** = mail/online order **T** = tastings and talks

Sunday Times Wine Club

New Aquitaine House, Exeter Way, Theale, Reading, Berks RG7 4PL
order line 0870 220 0020   fax 0870 220 0030   e-mail orders@sundaytimeswineclub.co.uk
website www.sundaytimeswineclub.co.uk   hours Mon–Fri 8–11, Sat–Sun 8–9   cards AmEx, Diners, Maestro,
MasterCard, Visa   delivery £5.99 per order   en primeur Australia, Bordeaux, Burgundy, Rhône.   C M T
✪ *Essentially the same as Laithwaites (see page 173), though the special offers come round at different times.*
The membership fee is £10 per annum. The club runs tours and tasting events for its members.

Swig

mail order/online only 188 Sutton Court Road, London W4 3HR (020) 8995 7060 or freephone 08000 272 272
fax (020) 8995 6195   e-mail wine@swig.co.uk   website www.swig.co.uk   cards Amex, MasterCard, Switch, Visa
minimum order 12 bottles   delivery £9.50 per address   en primeur Bordeaux, Burgundy, South Africa.   C G M T
✪ *Seriously good wines sold in an unserious way. For instant recommendations there's a list of 'current favourites' listed in
price bands; there's lots between £8 and £20 and the list covers pretty much everything you might want.*

T & W Wines

5 Station Way, Brandon, Suffolk IP27 0BH (01842) 814414
fax (01842) 819967   e-mail contact@tw-wines.com   website www.tw-wines.com   hours Mon–Fri 9.30–5.30,
occasional Sat 9.30–1   cards AmEx, MasterCard, Visa   delivery (Most areas) 7–23 bottles £15.95 + VAT, 2 or more
cases free   en primeur Burgundy.   C G M T
✪ *A good list, particularly if you're looking for Burgundy, Rhône, Alsace or the Loire, but prices are not especially low.*

Tanners

26 Wyle Cop, Shrewsbury, Shropshire SY1 1XD (01743) 234500   fax (01743) 234501
• 4 St Peter's Square, Hereford HR1 2PG (01432) 272044   fax (01432) 263316
• 36 High Street, Bridgnorth WV16 4DB (01746) 763148   fax (01746) 769798
• Severn Farm Enterprise Park, Welshpool SY21 7DF (01938) 552542   fax (01938) 556565
e-mail sales@tanners-wines.co.uk   website www.tanners-wines.co.uk   hours Shrewsbury Mon–Sat 9–6, branches
9–5.30   cards AmEx, Maestro, MasterCard, Visa   discounts 5% 1 mixed case, 7.5% 5 mixed cases (cash & collection);
5% for 3 mixed cases, 7.5% for 5 (mail order)   mail order delivery Free 1 mixed case over £90, otherwise £7.50
minimum order £25   en primeur Bordeaux, Burgundy, Rhône, Germany, Port.   C G M T
✪ *Outstanding, award-winning merchant: Bordeaux, Burgundy and Germany are terrific.*

Tesco

head office Tesco House, PO Box 18, Delamare Road, Cheshunt EN8 9SL (01992) 632222
fax (01992) 630794 customer service 0800 505555; 916 licensed branches e-mail customer.services@tesco.co.uk
website www.tesco.com hours Variable cards Maestro, MasterCard, Visa discount 5% on 6 bottles or more. G M T
• Calais store Tesco Vin Plus, Cité Europe, 122 Boulevard du Kent, 62231 Coquelles, France (0033) 3 21 46 02 70
website www.tesco.com/vinplus; www.tesco-france.com hours Mon–Sat 8.30–10pm
✪ *Premium wines at around £20 down to bargain basement bottles. Tesco.com has an even greater selection by the case.*

Thresher Group: Thresher Wine Shops, Wine Rack and Haddows

head office Enjoyment Hall, Bessemer Road, Welwyn Garden City, Herts AL7 1BL (01707) 387200
fax (01707) 387350 website www.threshergroup.com; 840 Thresher Wine Shops, 266 Wine Rack stores and 100
Haddows stores hours Mon–Sat 10–10 (some 10.30), Sun 11–10, Scotland 12.30–10.30 cards Maestro, MasterCard,
Visa delivery Free locally, some branches. G T
✪ *Australia, New Zealand and France take the leading roles, with strong support from Spain and Italy. The popular 3 for 2*
deal means you'll get some real bargains if you buy any 3 bottles – but some single bottle prices are on the high side.

Turville Valley Wines

The Firs, Potter Row, Great Missenden, Bucks HP16 9LT (01494) 868818
fax (01494) 868832 e-mail chris@turville-valley-wines.com website www.turville-valley-wines.com
hours Mon–Fri 9–5.30 cards None delivery By arrangement minimum order £300/12 bottles. C M
✪ *Serious wines for serious spenders.*

Valvona & Crolla

19 Elm Row, Edinburgh EH7 4AA (0131) 556 6066 fax (0131) 556 1668
e-mail wine@valvonacrolla.co.uk website www.valvonacrolla.com hours Shop: Mon–Sat 8–6.30, Sun 10.30–5, Caffe
bar: Mon–Sat 8–6, Sun 10.30–4.30 cards AmEx, Maestro, MasterCard, Visa discounts 7% 1–3 cases, 10% 4 or more
delivery Free on orders over £150, otherwise £9; Saturdays free on orders over £200, otherwise £15. G M T
✪ *A fabulous selection of wines from every region of Italy, including Sicily and Sardinia.*

Villeneuve Wines

1 Venlaw Court, Peebles, Scotland EH45 8AE (01721) 722500 fax (01721) 729922
• 82 High Street, Haddington EH41 3ET (01620) 822224

• 49A Broughton Street, Edinburgh EH1 3RJ (0131) 558 8441
e-mail wines@villeneuvewines.com website www.villeneuvewines.com hours (Peebles) Mon–Sat 9–8, Sun 12.30–5.30; (Haddington) Mon–Sat 9–7; (Edinburgh) Mon–Wed 12.30–10, Thurs 10–10, Fri–Sat 9–10, Sun 12.30–10 cards AmEx, Maestro, MasterCard, Visa discounts 5% per case delivery Free locally, £8.50 per case elsewhere. G M T
◗ *Italy, California, Australia and New Zealand are all marvellous here. Spain is clearly an enthusiasm, too.*

Vinceremos
Munro House, Duke Street, Leeds LS9 8AG 0800 107 3086 fax (0113) 288 4566
e-mail info@vinceremos.co.uk website www.vinceremos.co.uk hours Mon–Fri 8.30–5.30
cards AmEx, Delta, Maestro, MasterCard, Visa discounts 5% on 5 cases or over, 10% on 10 cases or over delivery Free 5 cases or more. M
◗ *Organic specialist, with a wide-ranging list of wines, including biodynamic and Fairtrade.*

Vin du Van Wine Merchants
mail order Colthups, The Street, Appledore, Kent TN26 2BX (01233) 758727 fax (01233) 758389
hours Mon–Fri 9–5 cards Delta, Maestro, MasterCard, Visa delivery Free locally; elsewhere £5.95 for first case, further cases free. Highlands and islands, ask for quote minimum order 1 mixed case. M
◗ *Extensive, wonderfully quirky, star-studded Australian list; the kind of inspired lunacy I'd take to read on a desert island.*

Vintage Roots
Farley Farms, Reading Road, Arborfield, Berkshire, RG2 9HT (0118) 976 1999 fax (0118) 976 1998
hours Mon–Fri 8.30–5.30, Saturdays in December e-mail info@vintageroots.co.uk website www.vintageroots.co.uk
cards Delta, Maestro, MasterCard, Visa discounts 5% on 5 cases or over delivery £6.95 for any delivery under 5 cases; more than 6 cases is free. Some local deliveries free. Cases can be mixed. Overnight is an extra £2.50 per case. G M T
◗ *Everything on this list is certified organic and/or biodynamic, from Champagne and other fizz to beer and cider.*

Virgin Wines
mail order The Loft, St James' Mill, Whitefriars, Norwich NR3 1TN 0870 164 9593
fax (01603) 619277 e-mail help@virginwines.com website www.virginwines.com
hours (Office) Mon–Fri 8.30–6.30, Sat 10–4, Internet 24 hrs cards AmEx, Maestro, MasterCard, Visa
discounts Regular special offers delivery £5.99 per order for all UK deliveries minimum order 1 case. M T

✪ *Online retailer with reasonably priced wines from all over the world. Well-balanced pre-mixed cases, or you can mix your own.*

Waitrose

head office Doncastle Road, Southern Industrial Area, Bracknell, Berkshire RG12 8YA
customer service 0800 188884, 193 licensed stores e-mail customerservice@waitrose.co.uk
website www.waitrose.com/wine hours Mon–Sat 8.30–7, 8 or 9, Sun 10–4 or 11–5
cards AmEx, Delta, Maestro, MasterCard, Partnership Card, Visa
discounts Regular monthly promotions, 5% off for 6 bottles or more
home delivery Available through www.waitrosedeliver.co.uk and www.ocado.com and Waitrose Wine Direct (below)
en primeur Bordeaux and Burgundy available through Waitrose Wine Direct. G T
• waitrose wine direct order online at www.waitrose.com/wine or 0800 188881
e-mail wineadvisor@johnlewis.com discounts Vary monthly on featured cases; branch promotions are matched.
All cases include a 5% discount to match branch offer.
delivery Free standard delivery throughout UK mainland, Northern Ireland and Isle of Wight. Named day delivery – £6.95 per addressee (order by 3pm for next working day). Now includes Sat. Next day delivery pre-10.30am – £9.95 per addressee (order by 3pm for next working day).
✪ *Ahead of the other supermarkets in quality, value and imagination. Still lots of tasty stuff under £5.*

Waterloo Wine Co

office and warehouse 6 Vine Yard, London SE1 1QL
shop 59–61 Lant Street, London SE1 1QN (020) 7403 7967 fax (020) 7357 6976 e-mail sales@waterloowine.co.uk
website www.waterloowine.co.uk hours Mon–Fri 11–7.30, Sat 10–5 cards AmEx, Maestro, MasterCard, Visa
delivery Free 5 cases in central London (otherwise £5); elsewhere, 1 case £12, 2 cases £7.50 each. G T
✪ *Quirky, personal list, strong in the Loire and New Zealand.*

Whitesides of Clitheroe

Shawbridge Street, Clitheroe, Lancs BB7 1NA (01200) 422281 fax (01200) 427129
e-mail whitesides.wine@btconnect.com hours Mon–Fri 9–5.30, Sat 10–4
cards Maestro, MasterCard, Visa discounts 5% per case delivery Free locally, elsewhere at cost. G M T
✪ *Half New World, half Europe, with some interesting selections hidden among the sub-£5 stuff.*

Wimbledon Wine Cellar

1 Gladstone Road, Wimbledon, London SW19 1QU (020) 8540 9979   fax (020) 8540 9399

• 84 Chiswick High Road, London W4 1SY (020) 8994 7989   fax (020) 8994 3683

• 4 The Boulevard, Imperial Wharf, Chelsea, London SW6 2UB (020) 7736 2191

e-mail enquiries@wimbledonwinecellar.com, chiswick@wimbledonwinecellar.com or chelsea@wimbledonwinecellar.com
website www.wimbledonwinecellar.com   hours Mon–Sat 10–9, Sun 11–7 (all stores)
cards AmEx, Maestro, MasterCard, Visa   discounts 10% off 1 case (with a few exceptions), 20% off case of Champagne
delivery Free local delivery. Courier charges elsewhere   en primeur Burgundy, Bordeaux, Tuscany, Rhône. C G M T
○ *Top names from Italy, Burgundy, Bordeaux, Rhône, Loire – and some of the best of the New World.*

Wine & Beer World (Majestic)

head office Majestic House, Otterspool Way, Watford, Herts WD25 8WW (01923) 298200
e-mail info@wineandbeer.co.uk   website www.majesticinfrance.co.uk

• Rue du Judée, Zone Marcel Doret, Calais 62100, France (0033) 3 21 97 63 00   email calais@majestic.co.uk

• Centre Commercial Carrefour, Quai L'Entrepôt, Cherbourg 50100, France (0033) 2 33 22 23 22   email
cherbourg@majestic.co.uk

• Unit 3A, Zone La Française, Coquelles 62331, France (0033) 3 21 82 93 64   email coquelles@majestic.co.uk
pre-order (01923) 298297   hours (Calais) 7 days 8–10; (Cherbourg) Mon–Sat 9–7.30; (Coquelles) 7 days 8–8. Calais
and Coquelles open Bank Holidays at the usual times. Free ferry crossing from Dover to Calais when your pre-order
is over £400.   cards Maestro, MasterCard, Visa. T
○ *The French arm of Majestic, with savings of up to 50% on UK prices. Calais is the largest branch and Coquelles
the nearest to the Channel Tunnel terminal. English-speaking staff.*

Winemark

3 Duncrue Place, Belfast BT3 9BU (028) 9074 6274   fax (028) 9074 8022; 79 branches   e-mail info@ winemark.com
website www.winemark.com   hours Branches vary, but in general Mon–Sat 10–10, Sun 12–8
cards Switch, MasterCard, Visa   discounts 5% on 6–11 bottles, 10% on 12 bottles or more. G M T
○ *Strong in the New World, with some interesting Australia, New Zealand, Chile and California.*

Wine Rack See Thresher Group.

The following services are available where indicated: **C** = cellarage **G** = glass hire/loan **M** = mail/online order **T** = tastings and talks

The Wine Society

Gunnels Wood Road, Stevenage, Herts SG1 2BG (01438) 741177 fax (01438) 761167 order line (01438) 740222
e-mail memberservices@thewinesociety.com website www.thewinesociety.com
hours Mon–Fri 8.30–9, Sat 9–5; showroom: Mon–Fri 10–6, Thurs 10–7, Sat 9.30–5.30
cards Delta, Maestro, MasterCard, Visa discounts (per case) £3 per collection delivery Free 1 case or more anywhere in
UK; also collection facility at Templepatrick, County Antrim, and showroom and collection facility at Montreuil, France, at
French rates of duty and VAT en primeur Bordeaux, Burgundy, Germany, Port, Rhône.
✪ *An outstanding list from an inspired wine-buying team. Masses of well-chosen affordable wines as well as big names.*

Wine Treasury

mail order 69–71 Bondway, London SW8 1SQ (020) 7793 9999
fax (020) 7793 8080 e-mail bottled@winetreasury.com website www.winetreasury.com hours Mon–Fri 9.30–6
cards Maestro, MasterCard, Visa discounts 10% for unmixed dozens delivery Free for orders over £200, England and
Wales; Scotland phone for more details minimum order 1 mixed case. M T
✪ *Excellent choices and top names from California and Italy – but they don't come cheap.*

The Winery

4 Clifton Road, London W9 1SS (020) 7286 6475 fax (020) 7286 2733 e-mail info@thewineryuk.com
website www.thewineryuk.com hours Mon–Sat 11–9.30, Sun and public holidays 12–8 cards Maestro, MasterCard,
Visa discounts 5% on a mixed case delivery Free locally or for 3 cases or more, otherwise £10 per case. G M T
✪ *Largest selection of dry German wines in the UK. Burgundy, Rhône, Champagne, Italy and California are other specialities.*

Wines of Westhorpe

136a Doncaster Road, Mexborough, South Yorkshire S64 0JW (01709) 584863 fax (01709) 584863
e-mail wines@westhorpe.co.uk website www.westhorpe.co.uk hours Mon–Thu 9–8, Fri–Sat 9–6
cards Maestro, MasterCard, Visa discounts Variable on 2 dozen or more delivery Free UK mainland (except northern
Scotland) minimum order 1 mixed case. M
✪ *An excellent list for devotees of Eastern European wines – especially Hungarian and Romanian – all at reasonable prices.*

WoodWinters

16 Henderson Street, Bridge of Allan, Scotland, FK9 4HP (01786) 834894
e-mail shop@woodwinters.com website www.woodwinters.com hours Mon–Sat 10am–7pm; Sun 1–5pm

cards MasterCard, Switch, Visa discounts Vintners Dozen: buy 12 items or more and get a 13th free – we are happy to choose something appropriate for you delivery £8.95 per address; free for orders over £150 UK mainland. Highlands, islands and Northern Ireland, phone for quote. en primeur Bordeaux, Burgundy, Italy, Rhone. C G M T
✪ *A young, ambitious operation, very strong on Califorrnia and Australia, but also good stuff from Austria, Portugal, Italy, Spain and Burgundy. They do like flavour, so expect most of their wines to be mouth-filling. Wine tasting club and courses.*

Wright Wine Co

The Old Smithy, Raikes Road, Skipton, North Yorkshire BD23 1NP (01756) 700886 (01756) 794175
fax (01756) 798580 e-mail sales@wineandwhisky.co.uk website www.wineandwhisky.co.uk hours Mon–Fri 9–6; Sat 10–5:30; open Sundays in December 10.30–4 cards Maestro, MasterCard, Visa discounts 10% unsplit case, 5% mixed case delivery Free within 30 miles, elsewhere at cost. G
✪ *Equally good in both Old World and New World, with plenty of good stuff at keen prices. Wide choice of half bottles.*

Peter Wylie Fine Wines

Plymtree Manor, Plymtree, Cullompton, Devon EX15 2LE (01884) 277555 fax (01884) 277557
e-mail peter@wylie-fine-wines. demon.co.uk website www.wyliefinewines.co.uk hours Mon–Fri 9–6 discounts Only on unsplit cases delivery Up to 3 cases in London £26, otherwise by arrangement. C M
✪ *Fascinating list of mature wines: Bordeaux from throughout the 20th century, vintage ports going back to 1904.*

Yapp Brothers

shop The Old Brewery, Water Street, Mere, Wilts BA12 6DY (01747) 860423 fax (01747) 860929
e-mail sales@yapp.co.uk website www.yapp.co.uk hours Mon–Sat 9–6 cards Maestro, MasterCard, Visa
discounts £6 per case on collection delivery £8 one case, 2 or more cases free. C G M T
✪ *Rhône and Loire specialists. Also some of the hard-to-find wines of Provence, Savoie, South-West France and Corsica.*

Noel Young Wines

56 High Street, Trumpington, Cambridge CB2 9LS (01223) 566744
fax (01223) 844736 e-mail admin@nywines.co.uk website www.nywines.co.uk
hours Mon–Fri 10–8, Sat 10–7, Sun 12–2 cards AmEx, Maestro, MasterCard, Visa discounts 5% for orders over £500
delivery Free over 12 bottles unless discounted en primeur Australia, Burgundy, Italy, Rhône. G M T
✪ *Fantastic wines from just about everywhere. Australia is a particular passion and there is a great Austrian list, some terrific Germans, plus beautiful Burgundies, Italians and dessert wines.*

Who's where

COUNTRYWIDE/ MAIL ORDER ONLY
Adnams
Aldi
ASDA
H & H Bancroft Wines
Bibendum Wine
Bordeaux Index
Anthony Byrne
ChateauOnline
Co-op
Devigne Wines
Nick Dobson Wines
Domaine Direct
Fine Wines of New
  Zealand
Roger Harris Wines
Jeroboams
Justerini & Brooks
Laithwaites
Lay & Wheeler
Laytons
Liberty Wines
O W Loeb
Majestic
Marks & Spencer
Millésima
Montrachet
Morrisons
Oddbins
OZ WINES
Real Wine Co
Howard Ripley
Sainsbury's
Somerfield
Stone, Vine & Sun
Sunday Times Wine Club
Swig
Tesco

Thresher
Vin du Van
Vintage Roots
Virgin Wines
Waitrose
Wine Rack
The Wine Society
Wine Treasury
Wines of Westthorpe
Peter Wylie Fine Wines
Yapp Brothers
Noel Young Wines

LONDON
Armit
Balls Brothers
Berkmann Wine Cellars
Berry Bros. & Rudd
Budgens
Corney & Barrow
Farr Vintners
Fortnum & Mason
Friarwood
Goedhuis & Co
Green & Blue
Handford Wines
Harvey Nichols
Haynes Hanson & Clark
Jeroboams
Lea & Sandeman
Moreno Wines
Philglas & Swiggot
Roberson
RSJ Wine Company
Selfridges
Waterloo Wine Co
Wimbledon Wine Cellar
The Winery

SOUTH-EAST AND HOME COUNTIES
A&B Vintners
Bacchus Wine
Berry Bros. & Rudd
Budgens
Butlers Wine Cellar
Cape Wine and Food
Les Caves de Pyrene
Flagship Wines
Le Fleming Wines
The Flying Corkscrew
Hedley Wright
Maison du Vin
Quaff
Turville Valley Wines

WEST AND SOUTH-WEST
Averys Wine Merchants
Bennetts Fine Wines
Berkmann Wine Cellars
Great Western Wine
Haynes Hanson & Clark
Hicks & Don
Laymont & Shaw
The Nobody Inn
Christopher Piper Wines
Reid Wines
Savage Selection
Peter Wylie Fine Wines
Yapp Brothers

EAST ANGLIA
Adnams
Budgens
Anthony Byrne
Cambridge Wine
  Merchants

Corney & Barrow
Hicks & Don
Seckford Wines
T & W Wines
Noel Young Wines

MIDLANDS
Bat & Bottle
Connolly's
Croque-en-Bouche
deFINE Food and Wine
Gauntleys
Harvey Nichols
S H Jones
Nickolls & Perks
Noble Rot Wine
  Warehouses
Oxford Wine Co
Portland Wine Co
Selfridges
Stevens Garnier
Tanners

WALES
Ballantynes
Fingal-Rock
Terry Platt Wine
  Merchants
Tanners

NORTH
Berkmann Wine Cellars
Booths
D Byrne
Great Northern Wine
Halifax Wine Co
Harvey Nichols
Martinez Wines
Nidderdale Fine Wines

Penistone Court Wine
  Cellars
Playford Ros
Richardson & Sons
Selfridges
Frank Stainton Wines
Vinceremos
Whitesides of Clitheroe
Wright Wine Co

SCOTLAND
Berkmann Wine Cellars
Cockburns of Leith
Corney & Barrow
Friarwood
Peter Green & Co
Harvey Nichols
Linlithgow Wines
Raeburn Fine Wines
Valvona & Crolla
Villeneuve Wines
WoodWinters

IRELAND
Direct Wine Shipments
James Nicholson
O'Briens
Winemark

CHANNEL ISLANDS
Sommelier Wine Co

FRANCE
ChateauOnline
Millésima
Oddbins
Sainsbury's
Tesco Vin Plus
Wine & Beer World